BEER

Edible

Series Editor: Andrew F. Smith

EDIBLE is a revolutionary series of books dedicated to food and drink that explores the rich history of cuisine. Each book reveals the global history and culture of one type of food or beverage.

Already published

Apple Erika Janik *Barbecue* Jonathan Deutsch and Megan
J. Elias *Beef* Lorna Piatti-Farnell *Beer* Gavin D. Smith
Bread William Rubel *Cake* Nicola Humble *Caviar* Nichola
Fletcher *Champagne* Becky Sue Epstein *Cheese* Andrew
Dalby *Chocolate* Sarah Moss and Alexander Badenoch
Cocktails Joseph M. Carlin *Curry* Colleen Taylor Sen *Dates*
Nawal Nasrallah *Eggs* Diane Toops *Game* Paula Young Lee
Gin Lesley Jacobs Solmonson *Hamburger* Andrew F. Smith
Herbs Gary Allen *Hot Dog* Bruce Kraig *Ice Cream* Laura B.
Weiss *Lemon* Toby Sonneman *Lobster* Elisabeth Townsend
Milk Hannah Velten *Mushroom* Cynthia D. Bertelsen *Nuts*
Ken Albala *Offal* Nina Edwards *Olive* Fabrizia Lanza
Oranges Clarissa Hyman *Pancake* Ken Albala *Pie* Janet
Clarkson *Pineapple* Kaori O' Connor *Pizza* Carol Helstosky
Pork Katharine M. Rogers *Potato* Andrew F. Smith *Rum*
Richard Foss *Salmon* Nicolaas Mink *Sandwich* Bee Wilson
Soup Janet Clarkson *Spices* Fred Czarra *Tea* Helen Saberi
Whiskey Kevin R. Kosar *Wine* Marc Millon

Beer

A Global History

Gavin D. Smith

REAKTION BOOKS

Published by Reaktion Books Ltd
33 Great Sutton Street
London EC1V 0DX, UK
www.reaktionbooks.co.uk

First published 2014

Printed and bound in China
by Toppan Printing Co. Ltd

A catalogue record for this book is available
from the British Library

ISBN 978 1 78023 299 7

Contents

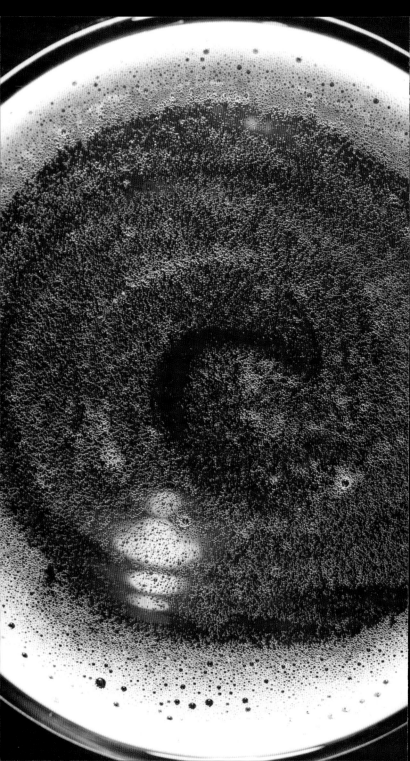

Introduction

It takes beer to make thirst worthwhile.
German proverb

Beer is the most popular alcoholic drink in the world, with a history stretching back perhaps as far as 10,000 BC, and with almost every country boasting some sort of brewing heritage. While other forms of alcohol tended traditionally to be limited in their spread and influence by climatic and geographical factors – you can only make wine if you are able to grow grapes – beer is ubiquitous and its essential ingredients, in one form or another, can be found almost everywhere.

The popularity of beer throughout the ages has been due to a number of factors. First is the aforementioned fact that it *could* be made, and second its comparative affordability, making it a drink for the everyman. Third, it had immense value as a drink that would not infect the imbiber with cholera, typhoid or any of the other diseases easily contracted from polluted water sources, at a time when clean drinking water was outwith the reach of many. Remarkable though it may seem from a modern perspective, from 1687 to 1860 patients at St Bartholomew's Hospital in London were each allocated three pints of beer per day, made in the hospital's own brewery.

Beer also had significant nutritional value – not for nothing has it been been referred to as 'liquid bread' – but perhaps its ultimate attraction has always been its intoxicating nature, imparting a feeling of relaxation and well-being, provided consumption is kept within sensible limits.

And that consumption, on a worldwide scale, is really quite remarkable. According to the *Kirin Institute of Food and Lifestyle Report* of 2011, during 2010 global beer consumption amounted to 182.69 million kilolitres, the equivalent of 288.6 billion 633-millilitre bottles. This was an increase of 4.33 million kilolitres (or 6.84 billion 633-ml bottles), or 2.4 per cent, over 2009, marking the 25th consecutive annual increase.

As we will see, the actual character of the beer consumed around the world has changed significantly over the centuries, as have methods of manufacture and the manner and occasion of its consumption. In the pages that follow we will not only chart the history of beer around the world, highlighting some of the greatest beer-making and beer-drinking nations, but also examine the drink's cultural associations and its versatility as an accompaniment to a wide variety of foods. We shall focus on the specific heritage of some of the globally best-known brands, not to mention indicating some of the best places to read about beer, find out more about its heritage and meet up with like-minded beer drinkers.

Beer has made a long journey from its origins in around 10,000 BC to the twenty-first century, but arguably there is now more diversity in, commitment to and passion for the subject than there has been for a very long time, and drinkers have lots of reasons for optimism. So pour yourself a glass of whatever style and brand takes your fancy, and join me as we explore the global history of beer.

I

Origins

He was a wise man who invented beer.

Plato

Like so many ancient crafts, the origins of brewing are some-what lost in the mists of time. A persuasive case can be made for the first brewers being Neolithic people in what we know today as Kurdistan – within the modern countries of Turkey, Iraq and Iran. These people were cultivating crops from around 10,000 BC and are thought to have developed the ability to make beer after accidentally discovering the malting process. Perhaps they dried grain which had become damp and started to sprout in order to preserve it, only to find that it released the enzymes essential to convert the grain's starch into fermentable sugars. Inevitably, qualifications such as 'maybe' and 'perhaps' occur frequently in any discussion about what happened so very long ago.

It has been suggested that brewing and other methods of creating alcoholic drinks probably developed independ-ently across Asia, Africa and the Americas, involving whatever grain crops or fruits were locally cultivable; there is an anthropological viewpoint that suggests nomadic lifestyles were sacrificed in order to cultivate crops, principally for the

Print of Ugandan Africans drinking millet beer, *c.* 1900.

production of beer. This is surely a possibility, given the
seductive powers of alcohol, once encountered!

The first nomadic hunter-gatherers to settle and grow
crops are thought to have been the Sumerians, who occupied
land between the Tigris and Euphrates rivers in what is now
Iran and Iraq. Regarded as the first really significant civiliza-
tion of the Middle East, the Sumerians invented the wheel and
the art of writing. Indeed, more than 5,000 years ago, they
recorded on a series of clay tablets a range of beer types and
recipes, contained within the ancient text 'A Hymn to Ninkasi'.
The name Ninkasi means 'the lady who fills the mouth', and
as well as being the goddess of brewing, Ninkasi was also their
goddess of fertility, harvest, love-making and the waging of
war. Ninkasi's nine children were each named after the potential effects of alcohol, including sons known as 'the brawler'
and 'the boaster'.

'A Hymn to Ninkasi' comprises a pair of drinking songs, dating from the eighteenth century BC, one of which describes the brewing process in detail, while the other praises the goddess for providing the opportunity for pleasurable intoxication. The work was discovered by archaeologists in the Sumerian city of Ur. According to the text, Sumerians made a double-baked bread called *bappir* from the grain they grew, going on to soak it in water to achieve natural fermentation, flavouring it with dates and honey before straining the resultant substance. Drinking was a communal activity for the Sumerians, who would sit round an urn of beer, drinking through reeds. It is claimed that wealthy Sumerians would carry personal drinking reeds decorated with gold, as status symbols.

Around 2,000 BC, the Babylonians conquered the Sumerian people, and ultimately brewing moved from being an entirely domestic occupation to a more formalized businesslike venture, intended to quench the thirsts of the civilian population and the army. As well as 'A Hymn to Ninkasi', the city of Ur yielded archaeological evidence of a large-scale public brewery, dating from between 2,000 and 539 BC. So important was brewing to the Babylonians that makers of inferior beer were sometimes drowned as a punishment.

The Babylonian king Hammurabi did much to formalize and categorize brewing, and in what is known as 'The Code of Hammurabi' he identified twenty different styles of beer, of which eight must be brewed using nothing but barley, while the other dozen might be made from other grains in any combination. Most prized of the Babylonian brews was spelt beer, while the Code also delineated wheat beers, red beers and black beers, not to mention a beer that was matured before sale, with a thriving export market existing in Egypt for this particular product.

The Egyptians were also notable brewers in their own right, and it is known that from at least 3,000 BC they were making a strong beer called *heget*, which used herbs, ginger, saffron and juniper as flavouring agents. For the Egyptians, as for the Babylonians and their Sumerian predecessors, beer occupied a role far more significant than simply that of a thirst-quencher or intoxicant. Beer was an important element in Egyptian medicine, and ultimately accompanied the dead into the after-life, being given as an offering to the gods. In the *Book of the Dead* there is a reference to *heget* being presented at an altar, while the Egyptian god Osiris was seen as the protector of those undertaking brewing, as well as being responsible for fertility, death and resurrection. Brewing was principally the province of women – a situation that was to prevail through many civilizations and across several continents until at least the end of the Middle Ages.

The thriving Egyptian brewing industry continued apace, even after Alexander the Great and his Greek forces invaded

Model of beer making from ancient Egypt. The two figures on the left are participating in the actual beer-making process while the ones on the right seem to be waiting to fill the vessels.

the country in 332 BC. In 430 BC the Greek historian Herodotus visited Egypt and recorded that 'The Egyptians drink a wine that they get from barley, as they have no vines in their country.' Subsequently, Egypt was under Roman control from 31 BC; like the Greeks, the Romans did not really understand the attractions of beer, being more in love with the grape than the grain. The Roman historian Tacitus wrote during the first century AD that the Germans and the Gauls were usually beer drinkers, while the Roman author and philosopher Pliny the Elder recorded the phenomenon of brewing in his *Natural History* (*c.* AD 77) as though observing a curious specimen through a microscope:

> The populace of western Europe have a liquid with which they intoxicate themselves, made from grain and water. The manner of making this is somewhat different in Gaul, Spain and other countries, and it is called by different names, but its nature and properties are everywhere the same.

Just as the presence of vines on their native soil made the Romans wine drinkers, so a lack of vines had led to the spread of brewing across Europe. Countries with cooler climates that could not support viniculture tended to be rich in barley and wheat. To the north, meanwhile, the Viking culture also placed great importance on beer, with brewing even taking place on board longships during campaigns of pillage, where one of its roles was to induce 'Dutch courage'. Viking warriors used the skulls of their slain enemies as vessels from which to drink their beer, and the Scandinavian toast 'skål!' derives from the word *scole*, which translates as skull. According to Norse mythology, the great hall of Valhalla serves as something approaching a convivial bar, where slain warriors carouse with beer which flows constantly from the udders of a goat called Heidrun.

In Europe, large-scale brewing came to be centred on monastic institutions; the patron saint of brewers, St Arnold of Metz, was an Austrian-born cleric who became bishop of Metz in northeast France during 612. Arnold recognized the link between dirty water and disease and repeatedly advocated the consumption of beer rather than water during his sermons. A year after he died in 640, in monastic retirement near Remiremont in Lorraine, his body was taken back to Metz at the request of the local population, and en route a refreshment break was made at Champigneulles. During the rest period it was announced that there was only one mug of ale left in the local tavern, and that it would have to be shared by everyone present. The miracle that led to Arnold's sainthood was that the single tankard never ran dry. He is also credited with declaring that 'From man's sweat and God's love, beer came into the world.'

Meanwhile, the monks of St Gallen in northeast Switzerland created what is generally recognized as the first commercial-scale brewery in Europe. Extant plans dating from 829 and an eleventh-century account of brewing in the institution paint a picture of a highly organized and sophisticated operation, with three separate breweries occupying a total of around 40 buildings. One brewery produced strong beer, known as *celia*, from barley and also often from wheat, for the exclusive consumption of the abbot and other senior figures in the monastery, along with important visitors. Meanwhile, the monks and visiting pilgrims were served with *cervisa*, brewed from oats and often flavoured with herbs in a second brewery, while lay workers and beggars had to make do with a 'small', weak beer, produced in the third brewery.

The process of boiling liquid and creating alcohol provided a safe alternative to water or milk, both of which were frequently contaminated with disease. The monks, their workers and their visitors would all have consumed the three types of beer regularly during the day, just as now we might drink tea or coffee. According to surviving records, in excess of 100 monks, 200 serfs and several hundred scholars from the monastery school were required to cultivate the cereal crops and brew the beer. Actual brewing took place in direct-fired large, copper brewing kettles, each of which was accompanied by a cooling vessel and a wooden fermenting tun. At that time, the process of fermentation was not understood from a biological perspective, and the action of yeast was widely seen as a miracle. Another miraculous discovery was the excellent preservative properties possessed by hops. Though modern drinkers tend to prize the 'hoppy' flavour of beer, there were many drinkers during medieval times who considered the bitterness of hops to be singularly distasteful.

It is known that hops were being cultivated in Bavaria during the ninth century, and an abbey hop garden is recorded in the Hallertau area as early as the year 736. Wenceslas I, Prince-Duke of Bohemia during the tenth century, considered hops so important that anyone caught exporting cuttings of hop plants faced the death penalty. The abbess Hildegard von Bingen, founder of the Benedictine nunnery of St Rupertsberg close to the river Rhine in 1150, wrote in *Physica* that hops, 'when put in ale, stops putrefaction and lends longer durability'.

Prior to the widespread use of hops as a beer preservative, the herbal mixture called gruit served a similar purpose, and also contributed positively to the drink's flavour. Gruit was made from a variety of ingredients, but bog myrtle seems to have been one of the most popular, along with yarrow. As the Catholic Church, along with members of the gentry, tended

Scourmont Abbey, Chimay, on a Belgian postage stamp, 1973.

to have a monopoly on the sale of gruit and indeed imposed taxes on it, ecclesiastical bodies had a vested financial interest in opposing the growing popularity of hops, but their spread could not be halted even by the forces of the Almighty and the establishment.

In addition to hops, monastic breweries were also responsible for another great innovation which, like the incorporation of hops, has stood the test of time. There was a long-standing problem with brewing during the warmer summer months, when fermentation became very difficult to control, with the risk of bacterial infection ruining the beer. Bavarian monks resolved the issue by storing beer for lengthy periods in cool cellars, which caused the yeast to sink to the bottom of the vessel and ferment in a much slower and more controlled manner than when it floated on the surface. This process of 'bottom fermentation' allowed beer to be stored for far longer periods than had previously been the case – the word 'lagering' was applied to this process, being derived from *lagern*, the German word for 'to store'. Essentially, all beer can be divided into 'ales' and 'lagers', though in modern times the terms 'ale' and 'beer' are often considered interchangeable.

As well as having had such a practical and far-reaching effect on the actual beer-making processes, monastic breweries continue to have an influence on the modern brewing world courtesy of a number of surviving monastic breweries such as the Trappist establishments of Chimay and Westmalle in Belgium, while the popular Leffe brand, though now 'outsourced' to a commercial producer, was first made in Leffe Abbey, near Dinant in Belgium, during the thirteenth century.

2

Beer in a Commercial World

While monasteries were very important centres of brewing, professional, secular beer-making activities spread across Europe, and during the mid-fourteenth century the German city of Hamburg was a world leader in brewing, though a series of catastrophic wars meant that it was really only during the eighteenth century that the production of beer on a commercial scale regained its former prominence. By that time, Germany's still surviving *Reinheitsgebot* or 'purity law' of 1516 was widely in force, specifying that beer should be made from only water, barley and hops.

In Britain, brewing was established as an organized, secular activity by the mid-fifteenth century, with brewers being granted their first royal charter of incorporation in 1445 by King Henry vi, which formalized a long-standing trade guild. The chronicler John Stow (1525–1605) wrote that in 1414 'one William Murle, a rich bruer and maltman of Dunstable, had two horses all trapped with gold', which suggests that there were enticing profits to be made from ale at that time.

Brewing also continued on a domestic scale in many countries, and was often the province of 'ale-wives' in Britain. Beer-making was an ideal occupation for women as it did not require a great deal of physical strength, and dovetailed well

David Teniers the Younger, *The Old Beer Drinker*, c. 1640–60.

with domestic chores, as significant periods of time had to elapse between the various processes. Additionally, the basic apparatus of brewing, including pots and vessels, would already be available within the household. The most successful domestic brewers ultimately began to brew as a means of making a living, selling their beer in what became known as 'public houses' or to operators of established taverns. Officially, the ale-wife had to place a pole with a bush attached in front of her house if she wished to sell surplus ale, so that its quality could be inspected by an official taster or 'conner', as they were often known. In many cases the conner would also be female, though most ale sold from domestic premises bypassed this official sanction, meaning that many transactions were illegal.

While ale-wives were plying their trade in Britain, across the Atlantic the first beer-making efforts of settlers in what was ultimately to become the USA were recorded by Richard Hakluyt, an English adventurer, in 1587. Hakluyt quoted a colleague, Thomas Heriot, as saying of Virginian corn that 'We made of the same in the country some mault [malt] whereof was brewed as good ale as was to be desired.' In Virginia, the colonists who established Jamestown survived first on supplies of beer brought on the voyage to America in 1606–7 and were then reduced to trading tools for beer with visiting sailors. It is recorded that in 1609 the governor of Virginia ordered advertisements to be placed for brewers to join the colony, but it was only twenty years later that there is evidence of two brewhouses operating in Jamestown. The best-known of all settlers in North America were the English Puritan Separatists, or Pilgrim Fathers, who travelled on the *Mayflower* in 1620 and made landing at Plymouth on Cape Cod, rather than along the Hudson River as intended. One of their leaders, William Bradford, wrote that the landing was made at Plymouth 'For we could not now take time for further search or considera-tion, our victuals being spent, especially our beer, and it now being the 20th of December.'

Meanwhile, in 1612, Dutchmen Adriaen Block and Hendrick Christiaensen established the first known truly commercial brewery in the New World in what was then New Amsterdam, now the Manhattan district of New York. Block and Christiaensen advertised in London newspapers for professional brewery staff to operate their enterprise. As the century progressed, brewing spread, with Philadelphia's earli-est brewery opening around 1685. However, many families in rural America brewed their own beer as part and parcel of the agricultural cycle, just as they also converted some of their grain crops into whiskey. Additionally, itinerant 'brew masters' would travel around the countryside from farm to farm with miniature breweries transported by horse and cart, undertaking brewing duties on behalf of the cereal growers.

Historically, most brewing was carried out on a localized basis, due to the difficulties of transporting bulky and weighty casks over long distances when roads were often of poor quality and only horse power was available for the task, though rivers were also pressed into service, and a significant number of breweries were located alongside waterways. However, while the finished product of the brewing process was not easy to transport, the essential grain ingredient was comparatively light and easily moved from one place to another, which meant that national malting industries tended to develop before national brewing occurred. The practice of malting barley – necessary to 'unlock' the starches which are converted into fermentable sugars – added sufficient value to the product to be worthwhile for businessmen to undertake.

Traditional brewing equipment.

It was only with the start of the Industrial Revolution during the eighteenth century and the rapid growth of areas of dense population, with the rise of urbanization, that widespread brewing on a large scale began to occur. As well as providing beer for increasing numbers of urban dwellers, the creation of networks of canals facilitated distribution on a much wider scale than had previously been feasible in most cases. The following century saw canals largely superseded by railways in countries all over the world, and these were even more effective in allowing barrels of beer to be carried across lengthy distances. The development of rail transport owed everything to steam power, and that power had already been harnessed by brewers during the later decades of the eighteenth century, following the patenting of a steam engine by James Watt in 1774. Just three years after Watt patented his innovation, Messrs Cook & Co. of Stratford-le-Bow near London became the first brewers to install a steam engine. In 1784 Samuel Whitbread acquired a steam engine to grind malt and pump process water in his Chiswell Street brewery in London, which had been built in the late 1740s.

The Whitbread operation was large in scale, turning out a remarkable 65,000 barrels of porter during 1758, but it was

Iced beer barrels being transported in a railway wagon, 1850–1900.

The brewhouse yard at the Whitbread brewery, Chiswell Street, London, *c.* 1791.

only one of many breweries created during the mid-eighteenth century to be equipped to produce the sort of quantities of beer that would have been unimaginable not too many decades previously. While Whitbread was the biggest brewer in London, Burton upon Trent in Staffordshire was home to a significant brewery established in 1777 by William Bass, and in Ireland Arthur Guinness developed his St James's Gate brewery in Dublin from 1759. Such brewers embraced innovative technology with the eagerness that characterized the age, utilizing hydrometers and thermometers, along with labour-saving devices that took much of the manual effort out of processes such as mashing.

In London, porter was the style of beer that reigned supreme. It took its name from the market porters who particularly favoured it, and was brewed from brown malts, using significant amounts of hops. Porter breweries installed vast vats in which the beer might be matured for several months. The investment in equipment was considerable, so porter production became the preserve of the more affluent London brewers, and established companies such as those of Barclay, Truman and Whitbread came to dominate the London porter scene. Porter was reputedly 'invented' during the 1720s by Ralph Harwood of the Bell brewery in Shoreditch and it consisted of heavily hopped, mild beer, which increased in strength during maturation.

Relatively fresh beer was blended with much older beer prior to sale, and the result was a product which kept well once distributed to retail outlets and was also comparatively cheap due to the large scale of production, hence its affordability among the capital's working population. In 1748 London breweries produced 915,000 barrels of porter, of which no fewer than 383,000 were credited to the city's dozen leading breweries. Porter's dominance only waned during the early nineteenth century when pale ales began to gain popularity. Pale ales – made from pale as opposed to amber or brown malts – had existed for at least a century before improvements in malting techniques, and particularly indirect kilning of malt, meant that brewers could rely on producing consistently pale-coloured beers.

George Hodgson, based in East London, was an early proponent of pale ales, which in character were light, sparkling and heavily hopped. At home, they began to attract drinkers from the burgeoning middle classes, and stylistically they were also ideal for consumption in the warmer climes of the British Empire, leading to a vigorous export trade. Hodgson began to send its pale ales to India in 1790, and the generic title India Pale Ale, or IPA, was soon in circulation. The focus of IPA shifted gradually to the established brewing centre of Burton

24

upon Trent in the English Midlands, with Samuel Allsopp making it there from 1822, and other Burton brewers such as William Bass soon added to the trade. Burton had long been noted for its hard water, which was ideal for pale ale production, though the town's brewing heritage dated back to around AD 1000 and the sort of monastic origins that characterized early, formalized brewing in so many European nations. From modest origins, Bass & Co. grew into one of the largest breweries and most ubiquitous beer brands in Britain. By the 1880s, Bass had built two new breweries in Burton, providing an annual output of close to 1 million barrels, and together the three Bass breweries employed some 2,500 people. The Bass 'red triangle' was the first trademark to be registered under the UK's Trade Marks Registration Act of 1875, as trademark number 1.

By that time, other technological advances had allowed brewers to expand and become more efficient, the most notable being the widespread availability of iron, which was much more durable than wood when used for vessels and tools and stronger than other available metals. This was due to ever-improving blast furnace technology – though blast furnaces had existed in China from about the fifth century BC. Concrete manufacturing had also been refined. As with iron making, concrete actually had ancient origins, with the Romans utilizing it in the building of aqueducts, bridges and even the dome of the Pantheon in Rome. However, it was during the nineteenth century that concrete once again came to be widely used in construction, and the brewing industry embraced it enthusiastically.

Meanwhile, the brewers of mainland Europe were developing lager brewing on a large scale, with Munich's Spaten brewery and Dreher's Viennese brewery offering light amber beers from 1841, while 1843 saw Josef Groll, working out of

Plzeň (also known as Pilsen) in Bohemia, produced the first pilsner, a golden lager beer. In 1873, Carl von Linde of the Spaten brewery invented mechanical refrigeration, using ether as the refrigerant gas to make large blocks of ice, following on from pioneering carried out in Australia to develop refrigeration apparatus two decades earlier, and this was a major factor in the ongoing growth of lager brewing. Around the same time as Von Linde was developing brewery refrigeration technology, the Frenchman Louis Pasteur was undertaking pioneering work that would lead to a true understanding of the science of fermentation, and how heat treatment of beer – pasteurization – inhibited the growth of microorganisms that spoiled beer and shortened its 'shelf-life'. His findings were published in 1876 as *Etudes sur la bière*.

Before long, the pilsner style was dominating the brewing world and being produced on several continents, with the USA being an enthusiastic producer of lagers, and only Britain holding fast to the tradition of 'ales'. To a significant extent, this state of affairs has remained to the present day, though the first purpose-built lager brewery in Britain dates back to 1881, when the Austro-Bavarian Lager Beer and Crystal Ice Company opened its brewery in Tottenham, North London.

3
Beer Comes of Age

By the latter decades of the nineteenth century, the processes of company consolidation and growth in scale of production that remain a feature of global brewing to the present day had begun in earnest. Increased processing efficiency and distribution methods allowed a smaller number of large breweries to make beer on an ever-greater scale, and in the USA, from a record high of 4,131 breweries operational during 1873 the number had fallen to around 1,500 by 1910. However, the volume of beer being turned out then was higher than in 1873.

In terms of takeovers and mergers, 1889 saw the Milwaukee-based firms of Franz Falk Brewing Company and Jung & Borchert join forces to form the Falk, Jung & Borchert Brewing Company. In turn, this organization was acquired by the Pabst Brewing Company four years later. Also in 1889, no fewer than eighteen breweries in St Louis, Missouri, merged to form the St Louis Brewing Association, and a year later the New Orleans Brewing Company was established from six individual breweries. In 1901, sixteen breweries in Baltimore combined to create the Gottlieb-Bauernschmidt-Straus Brewing Company.

Although we associate Prohibition in the USA with the period 1920–33, the crusade against alcohol had actually been established almost a century before, as the American Society

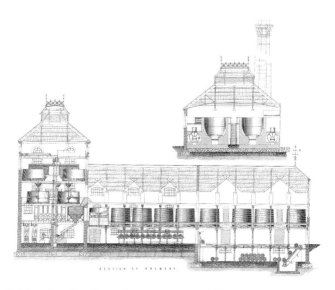

Building plans for a late 19th-century commercial brewery.

for the Promotion of Temperance had been founded in Boston during 1826. Prohibition had become law in the state of Maine in 1846, followed by several other states during the following decade, and long before the Volstead Act imposed national prohibition in January 1930, the temperance movement was a significant cause of concern for America's brewers.

Meanwhile, in Japan, American beers sold well during the mid-nineteenth century, before being eclipsed by British and German imports, and most Japanese brewing enterprises were initially owned during the nineteenth century by foreign interests. A truly domestic beer-making industry only developed during the last three decades of the century, when Japan's three largest brewing concerns were all established. Tokyo's Kaitakushi Brewery began production in 1876 and became the country's first Japanese-owned brewing enterprise, changing its name to Sapporo Brewery in 1886. The Osaka Beer

Brewing Company came into existence three years later, with a subsequent name change to Asahi, while the bankrupt Spring Valley Brewery at Yokohama reopened in 1885, going on to market the Kirin beer brand. In Britain, an apparently ever-growing demand for beer meant that by 1900 some 40 million barrels were being brewed per annum, though the temperance cause was also attracting support. Despite the growing levels of consumption, brewery numbers declined as in the USA, with the process commencing some years before, when national giants such as Whitbread & Co. started to absorb smaller rivals into their empires.

The years before the outbreak of the First World War in 1914 were times of economic recession, and more brewing company amalgamations and closures resulted. High levels of taxation imposed on beer, combined with reduced war-time opening hours for public houses at the behest of the Chancellor of the Exchequer David Lloyd George, who was noted for being anti-drinking, only served to exacerbate the situation. The result was that by the start of the Second World War in 1939 the 6,477 breweries that survived in 1900 had

Filling beer barrels, late 19th century.

Waiter with a bottle of Budweiser beer on a tray, late 19th century.

fallen to less than 600. Bottled beer became popular in Britain as public house drinking levels fell, and the significance of bottled beers was equally notable in the USA, where Adolphus Busch had commenced large-scale bottling operations at his Anheuser brewery in 1873. The practice of bottling beer is thought to have begun in the early eighteenth century, but it was really only in the 1860s that it developed on a significant scale, with corks being replaced by screw stoppers during the 1870s, and then by crown corks, which were patented in 1892. Bottling was undertaken by hand in laborious fashion until mechanization was introduced in the 1880s, and a new style of beer was pioneered specifically for bottling purposes. Known as 'adjunct beers', they were produced from sugar and unmalted cereals, which meant they remained 'bright' in the bottle for longer than beers made entirely from malt.

In the USA, filtration and artificial carbonation of bottled beer was standard by the turn of the century, though the practice of naturally conditioning bottled beer, where fermentation continues after bottling, remained popular in many other countries into the early 1900s. It is estimated that by 1900, some 20 per cent of U.S. beer sales were in bottled form and a decade later as much as 33 per cent of all German beers were bottled.

The first experimentation with canning rather than bottling beer was conducted in the late 1920s by Anheuser-Busch, Schlitz and Pabst in the USA, using very weak 'near beer', but

Collection of rare beer cans.

it was in January 1935 that the first flat-topped cans of Krueger Ale and Krueger Beer appeared on the market in Richmond, Virginia. Canned beer was an instant success, and in August 1935 the Pabst Brewing Company became the first major brewer to embrace the new technology. In Britain, the earliest company to introduce canned beers was Felinfoel brewery in South Wales, a year after they took America by storm, and though British drinkers did not embrace canned beers with quite the same initial enthusiasm as their counterparts across the Atlantic, there was no shortage of brewers eager to offer their products in metal rather than glass. John Jeffrey & Co. Ltd of Edinburgh soon produced a canned lager, while the London brewers Barclay, Perkins & Co. Ltd and Hammertons, plus Simonds of Reading and McEwan's and Tennent's in Edinburgh and Glasgow respectively, all followed suit.

Two world wars and unfavourable economic conditions across much of the world led to a slowing down in the momentum of brewery takeovers and mergers. But then the most rapid period of consolidation ever to have occurred within the British brewing industry took place, from the 1960s onwards. Joshua Tetley & Son Ltd merged with Walker Cain Ltd of Warrington in 1960 to form Tetley Walker Ltd, only for the new company to join forces with Ind Coope and Allsopp Ltd of Burton upon Trent and Ansells Ltd of Birmingham the following year to create Allied Breweries Ltd. By the late 1970s, six organizations controlled much of Britain's brewing industry. The 'Big Six' comprised Allied, Bass Charrington, Courage, Scottish & Newcastle, Watney Mann & Truman and Whitbread. By this time, Britain's traditional adherence to ale had given way to a new-found love of lager, driving ales into a minority position from which not even the vigorous activities of the pressure group Campaign For Real Ale (CAMRA), founded in 1971, could save it.

Around the world, the apparently relentless process of consolidation, amalgamation and rationalization continued, with the large-scale brewing of beer becoming concentrated into the hands of a decreasing number of global corporations operating a smaller number of vast breweries. For example, in the USA, Anheuser-Busch, brewers of Budweiser, has been owned since 2008 by the Belgian brewing giant InBev; now known as AB InBev, the company is the world's largest brewer. Meanwhile the large-scale Canadian beer producer Molson Breweries merged with Coors Brewing Company of Colorado in 2005, only to join forces with the South African Breweries Ltd-owned Miller Brewing Co. as MillerCoors in 2007. Across the Atlantic, AB InBev is also highly influential in the UK and mainland Europe beer markets through its ownership of brands such as Stella Artois, Jupiler, Hoegaarden and Leffe. The Danish brewing giant Carlsberg is another notably active European brewer, while Netherlands-based Heineken is responsible for brewing in some 125 breweries across 170 countries.

However, reactions against the perceived blandness and uniformity of beers produced by such international conglomerates has not been restricted to the activities of CAMRA in Britain, and small-scale 'craft' brewing operations have developed widely, with the concept of the 'brewpub', which made beer on the premises and renewed the long-lost connection between customer and brewer, being embraced with enthusiasm in the USA in particular during the 1980s and beyond. The first brewpub in the country was established by the Scots-Canadian brewer Bert Grant in 1982. Grant set up the Yakima Brewing and Malting Company in Washington state, which featured an on-site sales outlet as well as a small brewery, and soon the concept spread to California and New York. Beyond the brewpub was the small-scale professional brewer who sold beer to other retailers, and the USA now boasts a total of around

1,700 breweries, some 1,200 of which come under the 'craft' umbrella. Nonetheless, the scale of production remains modest, with craft brewers accounting for only 5 per cent of the total u.s. beer market in 2010.

In the same year Britain boasted nearly 800 breweries, though eight out of ten pints brewed in the uk emanated from breweries owned by either AB InBev, Carlsberg, MillerCoors or Heineken. Nonetheless, the dramatic growth in the numbers of independent brewers operating in Europe and North America during recent years illustrates the fact that an articulate and vociferous minority of drinkers crave flavour and individuality, innovation and regionality in their drinks, and the world of beer is all the richer for their presence.

4
The Art of Brewing

From the Babylonians to modern-day multinational brewing corporations, the fundamentals of brewing beer have remained much the same. While in days long gone by, our forefathers knew *if* something worked, today's sophisticated brewers also know *why* it works, thanks to the wonders of science. The first stage of beer making is to malt the cereal, whether barley, wheat, rye, oats or any other cereal. The process of malting involves steeping the grain in water before allowing germination to commence, then arresting germination by drying it in a kiln or roaster. During malting, enzymes convert the grain's starch into fermentable sugars, ready for the next phase of brewing. The drying process takes place at a range of temperatures, providing different styles of malt, from 'pale ale' malt to 'chocolate' malt, which in turn contribute varying flavour and colouring elements to the beer ultimately produced. Brewers will often use a range of malt styles when creating a beer, much as a winemaker will blend wines from different varieties of grape.

Barley remains the most popular cereal for brewing, principally due to the fact that it has a high incidence of the enzymes that convert starch to sugar compared to other grains. Consequently, a proportion of malted barley is usually employed along with any other cereal being used, in order to provide

Barley, the cereal used most in brewing.

effective conversion of starch to sugar. After the grain has been malted, the second stage of making beer is the conversion of starch into fermentable sugars in order to create alcohol. First, the malt is milled to produce grist, which is mixed with hot water in a vessel called a mash tun, resulting in a porridge-like substance known as 'mash'. Somewhat confusingly, water is always known to brewers as 'liquor'.

Mashing may occur by one of two methods, namely infusion or decoction. With infusion, the action of the hot water on the mash creates wort, a sugar-rich sweet liquid, which is drained off through slots in the base of the mash tun, while the remaining soaked cereal is sprayed with hot water – a process known as sparging – which removes the last vestiges of sugar. The spent grains, as the solids are known, are usually sold as animal feed, as they are particularly nutritious. The process of decoction is more usually employed for bottom-fermented beers such as lager, and entails draining off part of the mash and heating it in a mash cooker to a significantly

Pietra, a handcrafted beer from Corsica made from a mix of malt and chestnut flour.

higher temperature than that prevailing in the mash tun. This portion of the mash is then returned to the tun, and the temperature of the overall contents of the vessel rises appreciably. While infusion may last for up to two hours, decoction can go on for three times that duration and involves a lauter tun, equipped with revolving blades, which allows the wort to drain more effectively. Decoction extracts a greater amount of fermentable sugar than infusion, and this is necessary for the production of lager and other bottom-fermented beers due to their use of lighter malts, which contain less sugar.

The sweet wort that results from mashing is pumped to a copper or brew-kettle, which may be made of copper or stainless steel and is now usually heated by internal steam coils, though direct-firing, using flame provided by oil burners, remains in use in a small number of breweries. It is in the

Brewing coppers.

A hop plant (*Humulus lupulus*), the main flavouring agent in beer.

copper that the actual business of brewing takes places, with the wort being heated to boiling point, and here a vital ingredient in beer making is introduced, namely hops. Hops are available to the brewer in fresh, dried or pelletized form, and also as hop extract, though this tends to be disdained by most professional brewers. Hops added during the early stages of the 'boil' impart varying degrees of bitterness while also serving to clarify the wort. 'Late' hops are sometimes added towards the end of the boil, at which point their effect is principally aromatic.

It is difficult to overstate the importance of hops to beer character, and the influence they have varies significantly from

Loading a wagon with sacks of hops, early 20th century, postcard.

one type to another. Some beers are made with a single variety of hop, while others combine several, and it is the alpha and beta acids in each hop – the main acids in hop cone resins – that provide bitterness, while the alpha acids act as a preservative, and the hop's essential oils add aroma. Scientists and hop growers have laboured during recent decades to create more productive strains which have greater influence on ultimate beer flavour, just as barley growers have striven to improve both crop yields and potential alcohol yields. The result is that globally today's brewers have an extraordinarily wide variety of hops at their disposal, including Cascade, widely used in the USA to add distinctive bitterness and fruit notes to pale ales; Saaz, often favoured by European pilsner brewers; and classic hop varieties such as Fuggles and Goldings, which are at the heart of traditional British ales.

Depending on the style of beer being created, boiling lasts for between one hour and two and a half hours, after which the hopped wort is filtered through a vessel known as a hopback to extract the spent hops, and it is then cooled, usually by means of a heat exchanger. The wort is then pumped into fermentation vessels, where yeast is added, and the process of creating alcohol commences. The yeast proceeds to consume the sugars in the wort, creating alcohol and carbon dioxide. It is during fermentation that beer making takes one of two distinct directions. Top-fermented beers use specific yeast strains that rise close to the surface of the liquid, producing a foaming head, and fermentation usually lasts for between two and four days, with the yeasts being active at relatively high temperatures. Top-fermentation is used to make ales of varying kinds, as well as wheat beer, porter and stout. Bottom-fermented beers employ yeast strains that work at lower temperatures, with the yeast ultimately falling to the base of the fermenting vessels, and beers produced by bottom-fermentation are of the crisp, light-bodied lager style, and the period of fermentation is longer than with top-fermentation, usually between five days and a fortnight. A third form of fermentation, practised by a small number of brewers, notably

Traditional open-topped fermenting vessel.

in Belgium, harnesses naturally occurring 'wild' yeasts to create 'lambic' ales and Flemish ales, while a growing number of craft brewers have also seized on this method and have breathed new life into the genre.

Following fermentation (whether it has been top- or bottom-fermented), the 'green beer', as it is known, is pumped into conditioning tanks, where the carbon dioxide content is increased, which gives the 'head' on freshly poured beer. In the case of top-fermented beers, the conditioning period is relatively short, but with bottom-fermented beers it tends to last for a minimum of four weeks and often much longer, and takes place at temperatures close to freezing. Fresh yeast may also be added to induce a secondary fermentation. Prior to packaging, most beers are chilled and filtered, and 'dry-hopping' sometimes occurs. This involves adding dried hops to the conditioning tanks or even the casks, once they have been filled with beer, and the result is a more pungent aroma. Finings – made from the swim bladders of fish – may be added to promote clarity in the beer. In the case of most mass-produced keg, bottled and canned beers, pasteurization is also practised, and this process of heating the beer to kill off any bacteria which could sour the product and shorten its shelf life is often said to have a negative effect on the character of the actual liquid. There is no filtration in the brewing of 'cask-conditioned' or 'bottle-conditioned' beers, and additional sugar and yeast may be added so that fermentation continues in the container, adding to the complexity of the beer. With 'keg' beers, filtration removes the remaining yeast, thus preventing any further fermentation.

While many of the processes associated with brewing have not changed fundamentally over the centuries, the equipment being used has developed considerably. This is not to say that if you placed a medieval brewer in a state-of-the-art, mass-market u.s. or German brewery today he would be bewildered by what was happening, but there have certainly been significant changes over the centuries. Early mash tuns were simply small wooden tubs, with handmade hardwood paddles or 'mash-forks' (used to stir the mash on a manual basis), while the defining brewing stage took place in iron pots or hand-hammered copper vessels over open fires, where heating control was often erratic, resulting in significant variations from batch to batch. Copper is a better conductor of heat than iron, and steam heating of brew kettles makes for much greater consistency, as does the application of scientific principles and practices. These include the use of thermometers to monitor temperatures, hydrometers to indicate the strength of wort and beer, refrigeration and pasteurization. The pioneering microbiological efforts of Louis Pasteur led to a greatly enhanced shelf life for beer, while the Danish botanist Emil Hansen developed a means of growing yeast cultures that were free of other contaminating yeasts or bacteria, providing the Carlsberg brewery in Copenhagen with the first single-cell yeast culture in 1883.

5
Great Brewing Nations

Brewing takes place in virtually every country on earth, but it plays a more important cultural, social and commercial role in some than in others. Here we take a look at a number of the world's most significant brewing nations.

Belgium

Belgium is unquestionably one of the world's greatest brewing nations, not least because of the stylistic diversity of beers produced there and the sheer heritage behind those styles. The variety of Belgian beers is reflected in the number of different glasses recommended for their consumption, with pilsners requiring tall, slim glasses which retain the carbonation, while wide-topped, stemmed vessels are best for top-fermented ales in order to maximize aroma and flavour. Meanwhile, faceted glasses highlight the cloudiness and freshness of white beers.

The array of beers associated with Belgium is partly due to the fact that the country as it exists today has been ruled over and culturally and linguistically influenced by neighbours such as Austria, France and the Netherlands in times past. Brewing operations range from the artisanal and downright quirky to

Brewery in Rochefort Abbey (Abbaye Notre-Dame de Saint-Remy), Belgium, 2007.

Pieter Bruegel the Elder, *Peasant Wedding*, 1566–9.

the global reach of Stella Artois, though even that ubiquitous brand claims to be able to trace its origins back to a Leuven brewery in 1366. Modern-day Belgium only gained its independence from the Netherlands in 1831, but its brewing roots can be found in the Middle Ages. A Brewers' Guild was established in Brussels during the fourteenth century, and the Maison des Brasseurs in the city's Grand Place, which dates from 1698, replaced a much earlier building which served as the guild's headquarters. Today it retains its links with beer making, serving as a national museum for the industry.

Of all the beers produced in Belgium, the best-known are probably those classified as 'abbey' or 'Trappist', and they tend to share ecclesiastical links rather than a specific generic style. It is important to note that these terms are not interchangeable, as Trappist, or *trappiste*, is a legally enforceable appellation, granted in 1962 to those brewers conforming to strict guidelines. These include the stipulation that beer must be brewed within the confines of a Trappist monastery, either by monks or under their supervision; the brewery should not be profit-making, with all proceeds beyond the expenditure associated with brewing being donated to charity; and the beer itself must be of irreproachable quality. Of the seven designated Trappist breweries, six are located in Belgium and one in the Netherlands. The Belgian Trappist breweries category includes Achel, Chimay, Orval, Rochefort, Westmalle and Westvleteren. Despite the ancient origins of monastic brewing, all six of the Belgian Trappist breweries began, or recommenced, brewing operations during the late nineteenth or early twentieth centuries. Stylistically, Trappist beers range from Orval's golden ale through Westvleteren's blonde ale and dark beers to the 'dubbel' (strong and dark) and 'tripel' (strong and golden) ales of Chimay and Westmalle. What are termed 'abbey' beers are produced in commercial breweries which may or may not retain a link to an active monastic institution, and the most popular brands include Leffe, which is made in a variety of top-fermented styles, including the popular 'blonde' and 'brune' (dark) variants. Leffe beers are now brewed in one of Belgium's two Stella Artois breweries, in Leuven, with royalties being paid to the Abbaye Notre-Dame de Leffe by brand owners AB InBev.

Lambic beers are another Belgian speciality, now copied by craft breweries in a number of countries. Like Trappist beers, lambics are the subject of a strictly defined appellation, which governs production methods and imposes geographical parameters to their place of creation. The defining characteristic of lambics is spontaneous fermentation, and this ancient beer style has traditionally centred on the Pajottenland region of Belgium around the capital, Brussels. Lambics are usually brewed with unmalted wheat and malted barley, with a significant input of hops, but the hops used tend to be two to three years old and less aromatic and bittering than most employed in brewing, as their role is not to influence the flavour but to impart preservative properties to the beer. Fermentation takes place in shallow, open vessels which allow naturally occurring wild yeasts and bacteria to act on the wort, and before fermentation ceases the liquid is disgorged into wooden casks, where levels of acidity build up over time. Because so much is left to nature, rather than being governed by scientifically controlled input, there are significant variations between barrels, and blending is essential to create a uniform product.

In terms of character, lambics tend to be quite tart and challenging to many palates, and though they are made in relatively small quantities, they are beloved by many beer enthusiasts for their sheer individuality and the fact that they hark back to more primitive brewing times, before the chemistry of fermentation was properly understood. Some lambics incorporate fruit or fruit juice, such as cherries (*kriek*), and raspberries (*framboise*), while 'faro' is a sweetened lambic, designed for those who find the genuine article just too challenging. The purest, most traditional lambics are known as 'geuze' or 'gueuze', which comprise a blend of old and young lambics, usually presented in bottle-conditioned form, with ongoing fermentation leading to a significant degree of carbonation.

Lambics are often classified as 'wild beers', a genre that also includes Flanders red beer and Flanders brown ale. Flanders red is brewed using a red-coloured malt and undergoes a maturation period of nearly two years in large, wooden vats. Like lambics, this beer is characterized by the activity of *Lactobacillus* bacteria (a lactic acid bacteria) during fermentation, leading to a challenging, acidic fruit flavour. Flanders brown, sometimes known as 'sour brown' or 'oud bruin', also features *Lactobacillus*-type fermentation, and varies in colour from copper to deep brown. Both Flanders red and Flanders brown are usually a blend of older and comparatively youthful beers, with character varying depending on the proportions of each included.

Yet another beer style to be associated with Belgium is witbier, or 'white ale', though examples are also produced across the border in northern Germany. Witbier is characterized by the use of wheat, sometimes in combination with other grains, most often a small amount of oats. Belgian production of witbier was traditionally centred on Leuven and Hoegaarden, with brewing in the latter town dying out by the mid-1950s, along with the witbier style. Happily, it was revived during the 1960s by Pierre Celis, who had formerly worked in the last original Hoegaarden brewery of Tomsin. Today, the Hoegaarden brand is owned by AB InBev and the ingredients of this spicy, citric, refreshing beer include wheat, malted barley, hops, coriander and even peel from the lahara fruit, from which Curaçao is made. Hoegaarden is sold internationally, though smaller-scale examples of witbier are also produced by a number of independent Belgian breweries.

Germany

Mention 'Germany' to beer-lovers and their thoughts are sure to turn to Munich. The old capital of Bavaria is synonymous with brewing, and the first brewery in the city was established as early as 1269, while one dating from at least 1328, Augustiner Bräu, is still in operation, and has the distinction of being Munich's oldest brewery. It remains in independent hands while most of the city's other breweries now have links with, or are owned by, major international companies. One other anomaly is the Hofbräuhaus, which is in the hands of the state of Bavaria.

As well as breweries and a vibrant local beer culture, Munich is also home to Europe's greatest annual celebration of all things beer-related, the Oktoberfest. The festival attracts a remarkable 6 to 7 million visitors each year, and in excess of 6 million litres of Bavarian beers are consumed by them. The first Oktoberfest was staged in 1810 to celebrate the marriage of Crown Prince Ludwig, though the enthusiastic consumption of local brews did not become a focal point of the celebrations until eight years later. Today, beer drinking is accompanied by the provision of sauerkraut, bratwurst, oxtail and other traditional German foods guaranteed to soak up some of the alcohol. Six local breweries participate in Oktoberfest, namely Spaten, Augustiner, Paulaner, Hacker-Pschorr, Hofbräu and Löwenbräu.

Not only does beer occupy a place close to the hearts of the people of Munich and the whole of Bavaria, but the

Löwenbräu Beer Hall, Munich, at Oktoberfest.

Hofbräuhaus waitress, Munich.

southernmost of Germany's sixteen states is also an important
production area for several of the necessities of brewing life.
Bavaria actually cultivates around 35 per cent of the world's
requirements of hops, and also provides first-class brewing
barley and wheat, along with highly prized specialist malts.
From a historical perspective, brewing was certainly taking
place in what is now Germany during the Bronze Age, and
written records of German brewing exist from the Roman
era. As in so many locations, brewing beer became part of
monastic life, and the Benedictine abbey of Weihenstephan
began brewing under licence in 1040. Beer is still made there,
and the institution is generally considered to be the oldest
continuously active brewery in the world.

As secular brewing grew into an important industry, purity laws were developed to protect the integrity of the product, of which the most famous is now known as the *Reinheitsgebot*, or 'Bavarian Purity Law'. This term was actually first coined in 1918, though the origins of the legislation date from a decree issued by Wilhelm IV, Duke of Bavaria, in 1516, specifying the use in beer making of nothing more than water, hops and barley. Today, Bavaria maintains its own, strict, though amended, purity law, which restricts ingredients to water, yeast, hops and malted barley in the case of bottom-fermented beers, along with malted wheat and malted rye for beers that are produced by the top-fermentation process. The broader German purity law is more liberal, allowing for the introduction of sugar from external sources, and other variations on the Bavarian original. Both are enshrined in German tax legislation.

Germany is currently the fifth-largest beer producer in the world, where once it ranked second only to the USA. Today, China leads the way, followed by the USA, Russia and Brazil, and German domestic beer consumption has correspondingly fallen in recent decades, down by almost one-third in the last 30 years. Brewery numbers have dropped from around the 2,500 mark to just over half that, and the expression *Brauereisterben* (literally, 'brewery death') has entered the German language. During the nineteenth century, Berlin alone boasted some 700 breweries, a figure now reduced to around a dozen, while national beer output for 2011 fell below the 1,000 million hectolitre mark for the first time since reunification took place in 1990.

On the positive side, however, a developing craft brewing sector is helping to stimulate interest in traditional German beer styles, which have tended to become neglected as the relatively uniform pilsner product became dominant.

Indeed, pilsners – originally developed by a Bavarian brewer, Josef Groll, in what was then Bohemia and is now the Czech Republic – account for more than 50 per cent of the German market. However, weissbier – German for 'white beer' – is notably popular in Bavaria, and usually comprises 50–60 per cent malted wheat, being the equivalent of Belgium's witbier. A minimum 50 per cent of malted wheat is specified by law, and strong versions are known as weizenbock, while those brewed with darker malts are termed dunkelweizen, with *dunkel* meaning 'dark'. Probably the best-known brand of German weissbier is Erdinger, produced at the independent Erdinger Weissbräu brewery in Erding, which lies north of Munich. Despite having its origins in the Middle Ages, and traditionally being considered a proud, classic German beer style, weissbier lost its popularity during the twentieth century before experiencing a revival from the 1970s onwards. The variety now accounts for more than one-third of Bavarian beer sales, though nationally that figure is closer to 10 per cent.

Another German classic style is helles, which translates as 'pale', and like weissbier this is something of a Bavarian speciality, though also appreciated on a national level. The typical helles is straw-coloured, malty and mildly bitter, and is the staple 'session' beer of the Bavarian summer. Along with helles, dunkel is essentially a Bavarian lager style, but altogether darker in colour, hence the name, and to an extent dunkel has been usurped by helles in many locations, though it still enjoys popularity among the habitués of Munich beer halls and in some areas of Bavaria away from the capital. Dunkels tend to be moderately hopped, made using dark malts, and offer malty, toffee, chocolate flavours.

While weissbiers, helles and dunkels are not actually indigenous to Germany, altbier has its origins around the city of

Bock beer advertisement, c. 1882.

Düsseldorf, which is still its brewing heartland, though the 100-plus altbier breweries to be found in the city during the mid-nineteenth century have now dwindled to a much smaller number, largely concentrated in the ownership of major brewing organizations. *Alt* is German for 'old', the implication being that this is a traditional beer type, pre-dating the fashion for lagers. Altbiers are top-fermented, copper-coloured, malty and bitter in character.

Another indigenous German beer style is kölsch, which is also top-fermented and is produced in Cologne. This refreshing, aromatic, hoppy, golden beer appears in Cologne brewing records as early as 1250 and its ingredients, style and production locale are still rigorously defended by the Cologne Brewers Association, and around a dozen of the city's breweries continue to produce kölsch beers.

Bock beers originated in Einbeck, Lower Saxony, but today are more often associated with Bavaria. *Bock* means 'billy goat', and a goat's head often features on bottle labels of this strong, malty, bronze-coloured beer, which is usually bottom- fermented and traditionally seen as a winter speciality. An extra-strong variant of bock – known as 'doppelbock' – is produced on an annual basis in a number of Bavarian breweries for the period of Lent. Since this was a time of fasting, monks in the region traditionally brewed this 'liquid bread' to aid them in their abstinence.

Rauchbier is a rare German style of intensely smoky beer, associated with Franconia, and specifically the town of Bamburg. *Rauch* means 'smoke' – cured beech wood is used to dry the malt during kilning. The genre encompasses any beer made using smoked malt, but it is usually associated with lager of average strength.

Schwarzbier or 'black beer' is brewed using roasted malts, and, ideally, an amount of Munich malt. It is a bottom-fermented lager which is relatively dry, with toasted, dark-chocolate notes, medium-hopped and medium-bodied. The style had fallen out of fashion in pre-unification West Germany but retained its popularity in the East and, following reunification, schwarzbier has enjoyed something of a renaissance with German beer connoisseurs.

Great Britain and Ireland

The origins of beer in Britain are thought to date back to the fourth century AD, when the Anglo-Saxons arrived on British shores from what is now Germany, bringing with them the art of brewing. As in continental Europe, the monastic dynamic was at the heart of much British beer production, along with a modest domestic brewing culture. However, beer making developed into a more formalized and commercial industry

A view of Messrs Meux's brewery in Liquor-Pond Street, Clerkenwell, 1830.

from the fifteenth century onwards, and the eighteenth century saw a significant increase in the size of breweries in large towns and cities as the Industrial Revolution began to change the nature of British demographics.

The population of Britain was increasing, with more people living in urban environments. Gin had become so cheap and readily available that it was creating mass drunkenness, causing health and social problems, notably among women, hence the term 'mother's ruin'. Beer was promoted as a healthier alternative. Beer drinkers were also seen to be supporting British agriculture, and demand for the product grew rapidly. Many major brewers whose names were to become synonymous with British beer for more than two centuries set up in business during the eighteenth-century brewing boom. They included Allsopp, Bass, Charrington, Courage, Guinness, Meux, Whitbread, Worthington and Younger.

While the large London breweries initially concentrated on porter production, Burton upon Trent came to be associated

Worthington Brewery outing, early 1920s.

with pale ales. The water of the Staffordshire town percolates through gypsum rock, and small amounts of gypsum are dissolved as it does so. This makes the water rich in calcium sulphate, and the sulphate ions are partly responsible for the characteristic bitter, dry taste of the classic Burton style of pale ales. The calcium ions aid the conversion of starch into sugar during mashing, and later in the brewing process also aid the precipitation of solids – which produces a sparkling, bright beer.

North of the border, Edinburgh developed into the second-largest centre for brewing in Britain after Burton upon Trent; once again, this was largely due to the quality of the water which its brewers could tap into. An underground lake – known as the 'charmed circle' – runs from Arthur's Seat to the Fountainbridge district of the city, with an offshoot running into Craigmillar, and breweries were gradually developed along much of its course. The Scottish capital's hard, gypsum-rich water was ideal for pale ales, and 36 breweries were operating in Edinburgh by 1900, with the names of McEwan, Tennent and Younger to the fore. The town of Alloa, in Clackmannanshire, was also a significant centre for Scottish brewing, with George Younger's Candleriggs brewery leading the way in terms of scale. While researching the second volume of *The Noted Breweries of Great Britain and Ireland* (1889–91), Alfred Barnard visited Candleriggs and described Alloa as the 'Burton of Scotland'.

However, the number of breweries across Britain was already falling by the late Victorian era, due to several factors, not least a process of consolidation and rationalization as the largest brewers with national aspirations used their commercial muscle to take over smaller, regional operators, often closing down their breweries. One stubborn survivor was the Welsh brewery of Felinfoel, near Llanelli in the southwest, which was responsible for producing the first beer in Europe to be sold in a can. Remarkably, for a small, independent Welsh brewing operation, Felinfoel was beaten to a global exclusive with its canned product by only a few months, as the Americans just got there first.

Although Felinfoel managed to evade the clutches of acquisitive bigger brewers, the overall picture was bleak. In 1840 there were 50,000 breweries in Britain, but just 40 years later that number had decreased by half, and by 1900 less than 6,500 remained. When the Second World War broke out in 1939, the total had plummeted to less than 600, and numbers continued to fall during the subsequent half-century. By the late 1970s, half a dozen large organizations controlled much of Britain's brewing industry, with the 'Big Six' comprising Allied, Bass Charrington, Courage, Scottish & Newcastle, Watney Mann & Truman and Whitbread. Standardization was the name of the game, and cask beer began to disappear at a dramatic rate, being replaced by the keg alternative, where the beer is chilled, filtered and pasteurized before being served using artificial pressure. It keeps for longer and lacks the variability and unpredictability of cask ale, but also lacks a great deal of its character. The widespread introduction of keg beer was closely followed by British drinkers developing an enduring love affair with lager.

Today, large-scale brewing in Britain is controlled by four multinational organizations, namely AB InBev, Carlsberg, Heineken and MillerCoors, and the apparently ever-increasing concentration of brand ownership and product standardization has threatened to eradicate much that is unique and precious about British brewing and its stylistic heritage. However, the success of the Campaign for Real Ale (CAMRA) has been a refreshing feature of the past three decades and has provided a template for 'craft' brewers all over the world.

By the time CAMRA celebrated its 40th birthday in 2011, some 800 independent breweries were in operation across Britain, many ensuring the survival and revival of local brews, creating new takes on old favourites, and offering a significant degree of alternative choices to the mass-produced lager offerings of the global giants.

Perhaps the style of beer most obviously associated with Britain is bitter. Relatively dry and hoppy, served cool but not chilled, and of a strength to make it an ideal 'session' drink, bitter was the traditional staple of British pubs before the lager revolution and continues to enjoy a faithful following today. Bitter is a descendant of pale ale, but with the hop element toned down, and the term 'bitter' first appeared in print during the mid-nineteenth century. Tetley Bitter and John Smith's Bitter are the best-known mass-market brands, though many regional and craft brewers offer their own takes on the

A view of the malt tower at the Whitbread brewery, Chiswell Street, London, 1915.

style. Variants include the stronger and more complex Extra Special Bitter (ESB).

Pale ale is essentially a generic term that embraces bitter, India Pale Ale and other top-fermented beers that are made from pale malts, and British 'pale ales' were first brewed during the mid-seventeenth century. India Pale Ale (IPA) is comparatively high in strength and hop influence, both of which give it excellent 'keeping' properties and enabled it to survive lengthy sea voyages to quench the thirsts of soldiers and expats in India and many other outposts of empire. And quench their thirsts it undoubtedly did, as IPA is notably refreshing in character. For much of the twentieth century, as empire became a thing of the past, IPA declined in popularity across Britain, but it is a style which has found great favour with the craft brewing movement in recent years.

Like IPA, mild was a uniquely British style of beer that fell out of favour during the twentieth century, but while IPA has undergone something of a renaissance, mild remains a minority pleasure. Now generally taken to mean a dark-coloured, low-strength, very lightly hopped beer, the genre was originally a relatively young, mildly flavoured brew. Until the mid-twentieth century, modestly priced mild was at least as popular as bitter, with a strong following among working-class, urban drinkers. However, in that 'fan base' lay the seeds of mild's demise, as everyone in Britain suddenly seemed to aspire to middle-class status, and nobody wanted to drink something which conjured up images of ageing men wearing cloth caps, accompanied to the public bar by a whippet! Happily, craft brewers both in Britain and abroad have embraced mild, albeit to a modest extent, and the old soldier is still alive and kicking.

Stout has also gained popularity with small-scale brewers in recent years, though its mainstream Irish producers, namely Guinness, Murphy's and Beamish, represent the bulk of sales.

This is 'dry stout' or 'Irish stout', almost black in colour, and made with a percentage of roasted malt, leading to its characteristic dry, coffee-like notes. Stout has its origins in porter, and indeed it was originally called 'stout porter', denoting a significant degree of strength. It came to have the generic sense of any strong beer, before becoming associated with the specific style we now identify so closely with Ireland and Irish drinking. For many people, stout *is* Guinness, and the genre prospered in Dublin partly because the city's water was ideally suited to the brewing of dark beers. By the 1880s the

Dublin Guinness brewery of St James's Gate was the largest in the world, and although Ireland was far from immune to the lager revolution of the second half of the twentieth century, Guinness in particular has managed to brand itself as a traditional drink that young people are proud to be seen consuming. Its international following has developed thanks to the marketing muscle and reach of its parent company, Diageo plc.

Other variations on the stout theme include oatmeal stout, in which a proportion of oatmeal is included alongside malted barley, leading to a voluptuous mouth-feel. Oatmeal stout was a big seller during the Victorian era, when stouts in general were at their height of popularity, since they were often perceived as having properties beneficial to nutrition and of value to the sick. Another member of the stout family is Russian or imperial stout, which was conceived in eighteenth-century London as a very strong porter for the export trade, particularly the Baltic countries. It was reputed to be a favourite of the Russian empress Catherine the Great.

Barley wine tends to crank up the strength even higher than imperial stout, and its origins lie in the private breweries of large houses during the eighteenth century. Initially barley wines were produced using dark malts, but later, as commercialization took over, pale malts came to predominate, and lengthy ageing has always been a feature of this relatively expensive beer. Barley wines tend to be sweet, intense and fruity in character. Barley wine is closely related to old ale, or strong ale, and as with traditional barley wine, the brewing process employed only the early 'runnings' of the mash, which were very strong. Old ales, stored in wooden casks for months or even years, were often blended with younger, fresher beers to create a rich, complex and livelier product. Modern 'old ales' tend to undergo shorter periods of ageing than their forebears and the term is often applied simply to a brewer's fuller-bodied, sweet, dark, higher strength, seasonal winter brews.

A beer term peculiar to Scotland is 'heavy', which is essentially a medium-strength bitter, while stronger versions are known as 'export' or 'special'. A 'wee heavy' is stronger still, often with an ABV in excess of 7 per cent. Historically, Scottish beers tended to be less heavily hopped than their English counterparts, principally due to the long distance between Scotland's breweries and the nearest hop-growing areas. Scotland is also notable for its use of the 'shilling' terminology to denote beer strength. This system was brought in after the introduction of Beer Duty in 1880, with the 'shillings' originally being the price per barrel before tax, but over time they came to serve merely as an indicator of the strength and type of beer, with pale ale being 50 to 60 shillings, while 'export' was 70 to 80 shillings. The most widely available example is Caledonian 80 Shillings, produced in the last surviving full-scale brewery in Edinburgh.

USA

European settlers carried the craft of brewing beer with them to the New World in the late sixteenth and early seventeenth centuries, and a commercial brewery was established in what is now New York as early as 1620. More dedicated breweries sprung up across the country during the rest of the century, creating the beginnings of a nationwide industry. However, British colonists and those of British descent who might have been expected to establish brewing on a firm footing, did not really make their mark to any significant degree. Instead, it was German migrants who arrived in large numbers from the 1830s

Philadelphia brewery, *c.* 1870.

onwards who really carried the business of brewing forward in a truly dynamic way.

Ales and porters were produced by America's brewers until one John Wagner arrived in Philadelphia from Bavaria in 1840, carrying with him a bottom-fermenting yeast with which lager could be made. Soon, lager had replaced ale and porter in the affections of most Americans, a development due in no small part to the growing Germanic demographic. In total, some 8 million Germans settled in the USA during the nineteenth century. And it was Germans who were responsible for creating many of the great American brewing companies which dominated beer making during the twentieth century, and which survive in mutated forms to this day.

For example, Eberhard Anheuser migrated from his native Bad Kreuznach in west Germany to the USA, settling in St Louis, Missouri, in 1842. He made his fortune through a soap factory which he established, entering the brewing business effectively by accident when a major creditor was unable to pay Anheuser, handing over his brewery to settle the debt. Thus, the Bavarian Brewing Company became E. Anheuser & Co., and

The Anheuser-Busch Brewery at Broadway and Pestalozzi, St Louis, Missouri, *c.* 1900.

in March 1861 Anheuser's daughter married Adolphus Busch, who originated in Mainz, and who owned a brewing supply company. Clearly, two matches were made in heaven with the union, and Busch went on to join his father-in-law's business, which ultimately became known as Anheuser-Busch. Their Czech-style Budweiser brand was introduced in 1876. Today,

Budweiser delivery in Washington, DC, 1920s.

the famous old brewer is part of the largest beer company in the world, AB InBev, with headquarters in Belgium, though it operates a dozen breweries across the U.S., turning out a total close to 100 million barrels per annum and accounting for nearly half of all domestic beer consumption. There has, however, been a dispute, lasting for more than a century, between the owners of the U.S. Budweiser brand and the owners of Budweiser Budvar, produced in the Czech Republic city of Budweis, over use of the 'Budweiser' name, though an accommodation of sorts has now been reached.

Meanwhile, Adolph Coors, or Kuhrs, was another German who migrated to the USA, arriving in 1868 and finally settling in Denver, Colorado, four years later. Unlike Eberhard Anheuser, Coors was a brewer by trade, with beer-making experience in his homeland, and he established a brewery in Golden, Jefferson County, at the foot of the Rocky Mountains, operating a partnership with one Jacob Schueler. In 1880 he bought

Red Stripe Light. Although it's known as a Jamaican brand, the Red Stripe company originated in Galena, Illinois. It's now owned by Diageo.

out his partner and the brewery became known as Adolph Coors Golden Brewery. During the 1980s, Coors spread out of its western heartland states to develop a significant national presence, going on to acquire the UK brewing interests of Bass Brewers Ltd of Burton upon Trent in 2002, before merging with the Canadian Molson Brewing Company three years later. Coors brewery at Golden in Colorado is the largest brewery in the world, with an annual capacity of around 20 million barrels per year.

Since 2008, Coors has operated in the USA through a joint venture with SABMiller, known as MillerCoors. The Miller Brewing Company was also founded by a German migrant, Frederick Miller, originally Friedrich Müller, from Riedlingen, who arrived in the USA in 1854, acquiring a brewery close to Milwaukee, Wisconsin, the following year. Ultimately the Miller brand – focused around Miller Lite, the first commercially successful low-calorie beer – became the second-best seller behind Budweiser in the domestic market, and was purchased by South African Breweries Ltd (SAB) in 2002, leading to the creation of SABMiller. Miller now brews in six states across the USA, with 'Miller Valley' in Milwaukee remaining the 'brand home', featuring a replica of the original Plank Road brewery, which is a popular tourist attraction. Milwaukee was also home to the Joseph Schlitz Brewing Company, at one time the largest beer producer in the world. It used the advertising slogan 'The beer that made Milwaukee famous', a tagline that inspired the popular beer-related song 'What Made Milwaukee

Great Pabst Brewery, Milwaukee, 1909, postcard. Note the changes since 1844, as depicted at top left.

749 cases of beer (18,000 bottles) being destroyed in the District of Columbia during Prohibition, 1923.

Famous', which was a hit for Jerry Lee Lewis in 1968 and was subsequently successfully covered by Rod Stewart.

Brewers in the USA faced a crisis during the early twentieth century that their European compatriots did not have to deal with, namely the imposition of Prohibition. Localized prohibition of alcohol manufacture dated back to 1850, when the state of Maine went 'dry', but in January 1920 the Volstead Act made Prohibition a nationwide reality, at which time there were almost 1,200 breweries operating across the USA. During Prohibition breweries were forced to diversify in order to remain in business, with Coors, for example, moving into non-alcoholic beer and malted milk production, while Anheuser-Busch also made non-alcoholic beer, along with refrigerated cabinets. 'Near beer', with a strength of 0.5 per cent alcohol, was also produced by many breweries. Prohibi-tion was lifted in 1933 and brewing began again, with Coors's brewery recommencing beer making at midnight on 7 April 1933, the exact minute when alcohol production became legal once more. However, three years later only 700 breweries were functioning. Brewery numbers continued to fall steeply during the half-century after repeal, due to the same sort of consolidation of ownership that was occurring in manufacturing industries all over the world, and by 1984 only 83 breweries were open for business, owned by just 44 brewers. This was a remarkably low figure for a country where beer consumption had risen and there was a total population of some 222 million people.

While beers produced by AB InBev and SABMiller now account for a very high percentage of all domestic beer consumption, the U.S. beer scene has been characterized in recent years by a thriving craft brewing movement, which has developed as a reaction against the ubiquity of a small number of brands and a perception of blandness within those brands. One of the earliest craft brewing pioneers was Fritz Maytag, who purchased a majority interest in the near-bankrupt Anchor

Anchor Brewery, San Francisco, c. 1905.

Brewing Company in San Francisco in 1965, going on to revive Anchor Steam Beer. This is fermented in shallow, open fermenters and had its origins back in 1896, first being released in bottled format by Maytag in 1971. Soon other small-scale, independently minded brewers followed Maytag's example, and eventually the trickle became a veritable flood, with three times as many operational breweries by 1990 as there had been little more than a decade earlier. Today the number has risen to around 1,700, though craft beers account for only some 5 per cent of U.S. beer sales, with imported beers making up another 13 per cent, as American drinkers seek something slightly different to their usual 'Bud' or Miller Lite.

The craft brewers of the USA major in big, bold flavours and have taken much of their inspiration from Europe, with several dedicated Belgian-style breweries now operating, and innovation and experimentation are at the forefront of much craft brewing. At its most extreme this has led to some bizarre brews, with the Cambridge Brewing Company's Boston brewery-restaurant producing a beer which was aged for a year in Napa Valley French oak wine barrels and contained grapes and apricots!

Rest of the World

Beer of some sort is brewed in almost every country in the world, and when it comes to the 'league table' of leading beer-producing and beer-consuming countries, there are some surprises to be found. After being world leader for so many decades, the USA has now fallen into second place behind China. Indeed, China now accounts for almost 25 per cent of the global beer market. Brewing was taking place in China up to 9,000 years ago, but it is only with the country's emergence

The Thai
beer Singha.

as a major economic player on the world stage during the last two decades that dramatic beer-related growth figures have emerged. More than 500 breweries are in production in China, and the most significant Chinese brewers tend to be involved in joint ventures with major overseas brewing corporations. However, some of those corporations, such as Carlsberg, which owns or part-owns no fewer than 47 breweries across China, are investing on a major scale in the Chinese brewing market

Sapporo, a
Japanese brand.

in their own right, and Carlsberg has a lengthy relationship with China, first exporting beer to the country back in 1876.

Third in the global league table of beer consumption is Brazil, a country which has enthusiastically embraced the craft beer revolution in recent years, with some 100 craft breweries now active, though AB InBev accounts for two-thirds of all beer drunk nationally. Dutch colonists carried the art of brewing with them to Brazil in 1634. Behind Brazil comes Russia, whose beer market is dominated by the Carlsberg-owned Baltika Breweries, which runs ten breweries in Russia, with Moscow and St Petersburg as its principal hubs.

Entrance to Prazdroj Brewery, Pilsen, Czech Republic.

Although only occupying 23rd place among the statistics of beer consumption by volume, the Czech Republic boasts some 125 breweries, and the per-head drinking figure is 160 litres per year, double that of the USA. The Czech Republic also occupies an important historical place in brewing as the originator of the pilsner style.

Australia has a brewing heritage which is British in origin, with a number of large-scale indigenous brewing companies becoming active during the nineteenth century. Today, Carlton United Brewers (CUB) is the largest player in the Australian beer market, being responsible for iconic brands such as Victoria Bitter and Foster's, with the latter dating back to 1888 in Melbourne when two American brothers, William and Ralph Foster, began to brew beer. CUB is, in turn, owned by SABMiller. Along with Foster's, another famous Australian beer brand is Tooheys of Sydney, which was established in 1860. Today, Tooheys is part of Lion Nathan National Foods, owned by the

Japanese drinks firm Kirin Holdings Company Ltd, and Lion Nathan is also responsible for the high profile Castlemaine xxxx, which it brews in Brisbane.

Mexico's brewing industry is dominated by Grupo Modelo, part-owned by AB InBev, and Heineken Mexico, formerly FEMSA Cerveza. The two companies principally produce pilsner-style beers very similar to those that predominate across the border in the USA, but historically, brewing in Mexico was shaped by Austrian and German influences. During the reign of Emperor Maximiliano I (r. 1864–7), who had been born in Austria, many Austrians and Germans settled in Mexico, taking with them brewing skills, which they put to good use. By the early 1900s there were some 35 breweries in Mexico, but the last century has seen the same sort of consolidation that has been a trademark of the brewing industry all over the world.

The Scandinavian countries of Denmark, Norway and Sweden all boast fascinating brewing heritages, with their

Elephant Tower, Carlsberg Brewery, Copenhagen.

Castle Brewery, Pretoria, South Africa, late 19th century.

northern location ruling out viticulture and a native wine-
drinking tradition. Beer making in Denmark is thought to
date from around 1370 BC, and there was a strong monastic
brewing culture in the Middle Ages, while by the end of the
seventeenth century the capital of Copenhagen boasted some
140 breweries. With the founding of the Carlsberg brewery
in 1847, a lager-drinking culture was established in Denmark
and its ubiquity has lessened only in recent years with the
development of a thriving craft brewing sector. Brewing in
Norway dates from around the start of the thirteenth century,
and during the seventeenth and eighteenth centuries it was
actually compulsory for landowners to brew beer. Commercial
brewing began later than in Denmark, really only starting during the first half of the nineteenth century, though by 1857 the
country had more than 350 operational breweries, and dark,
Bavarian-style lagers were popular until after the Second
World War, when pilsner became the dominant style.

Beer is known to have been brewed in what is now Sweden as early as the Nordic Bronze Age, which lasted from 1700 from 500 BC, and hops were first introduced around AD 1100, with peasants being required by law to cultivate hops from 1442 to 1734 in order to reduce dependency on imports. As in so many other countries, lager became the dominant style in Swedish brewing from the mid-nineteenth century onwards.

6

Drinking Beer

Inevitably, with such an age-old pursuit as the consumption of beer and the frequently convivial, communal aspects pertaining to that consumption, traditions, customs, rituals and practices have developed all over the world, some of which are international in application, while others remain remarkably localized. The places in which consumption takes place also vary quite significantly, and when it comes to drinking beer, no other country can boast an institution quite like the British pub.

According to Frederick Hackwood in *Inns, Ales and Drinking Customs of Old England* (1909), 'certain it is that inns made their appearance in this country with the very earliest dawn of civilisation'. He notes that when the Romans arrived in Britain after AD 43 and began their famous programmes of road building, they sited alongside them 'houses of entertainment for man and horse, which were the Roman equivalent for, and prototype of, the good old English wayside hostelry . . . The English inn, as equivalent to a drinking-shop, was not [established] till the advent of the English [nation].' He observes that by the seventh century there were the equivalent of alehouses in Britain, while the 'Laws' of King Æthelbert of Kent of 616 contain regulations regarding 'eala-hus'.

Ye Olde Fighting Cocks, St Albans, 1930s. The Cocks has a strong claim to the title of the oldest public house in England.

In 1577, a census recorded the existence of 19,759 inns, taverns and alehouses in England and Wales. With a total population of 3.7 million, that equated to a remarkable figure of one place of 'refreshment' for every 187 people. Hackwood notes that an act passed during the first year of the reign of King James I in 1603 defined 'the antient, true, and principal use of inns, ale-houses, and victualling houses' to be for the 'resort, relief, and lodging of wayfaring people, travelling from place to place, and for such supply of the wants of such people as are not able by greater quantities to make provision of victual'. The preamble then proceeds to lay down that such inns 'are not meant for entertainment and harbouring of lewd idle people, to spend and consume their time and their money in lewd and drunken manner'.

During the Victorian era, many brewers began to purchase retail outlets of their own rather than sell beer to independent licensees. This notion of 'tied houses' developed as fierce competition raged between rival brewers. Owning outlets provided guaranteed sales, and in addition to purchasing existing public houses, brewers also embarked on programmes of construction, with new hostelries often being designed along rather grand and sumptuous lines. Between 1886 and 1900 no fewer than 234 breweries went public in order to raise funds, principally to enable them to acquire or build public houses.

British public houses changed remarkably little during the twentieth century until after the Second World War. Then, during the 1960s and '70s, brewers realized that they had to do more to get people into their pubs and, in particular, attract uncommitted drinkers. Food, entertainment and overall ambience tended to become more important than the variety and quality of beer on offer. In recent years, however, as social habits have changed, the very existence of many pubs has been threatened, particularly in rural areas, despite the introduction of more liberal licensing laws allowing for the option of all-day opening.

A significant development of the last three decades has been the retreat of many larger brewing companies from 'vertically integrated' operations, with their breweries serving a core market of managed or 'tenanted' public houses. Great names such as Bass and Whitbread as well as a host of regional brewers have abandoned brewing entirely in order to concentrate solely on operating licensed premises and other leisure enterprises. Their beers and lagers are now brewed for them under contract by third parties, thus destroying the historic links between brands and locality. This has led to the rise in what are often termed 'pub companies' or 'pubcos', which have now almost replaced brewers as the principal retailers of beer in Britain. Two of the largest currently operating are Punch Taverns and Enterprise Inn, each of which own in excess of 6,000 premises.

Some 57,000 pubs currently operating in the UK, of which 'pubcos' and regional brewers own around 30,000, and while 57,000 may seem like a lot of pubs, British licensed premises were closing at a rate of 25 per week during 2012, with the problem at its worst in rural areas. The smoking ban, imposed across England, Wales and Northern Ireland during 2007, a year after it became law in Scotland, has served to exacerbate existing obstacles to the flourishing of the public house, which include the ready availability of cheap, supermarket beer, more sophisticated home entertainment systems and drink-driving laws. The problem is not unique to Britain, either, with the great beer-drinking nation of Germany suffering from falling consumption levels across the board and less busy drinking venues as a result. The largest beer hall in Munich used to be the 5,000-seat Mathäser, but it has now been demolished and replaced with a multiplex cinema. According to Christian DeBenedetti, in a feature on Slate.com in March 2011,

These days, Germany's celebrated brewing towns and atmospheric old taverns can feel like retirement homes. Visitors to the south of Germany today (where more than half the nation's breweries are located) find few of the ardent young beer lovers that crowd craft watering holes in Copenhagen; Brussels; London; New York; Portland, Ore.; and even Rome. And while it's true that last fall's 200th Oktoberfest was bigger than ever, using Oktoberfest to measure the health of German beer culture is like using Disney World admissions to measure the health of American cinema. Once a decorous wedding pageant, Oktoberfest is a hot mess, with cheesy carnival rides and hordes chugging cheap lager as if it were Hawaiian Punch. Paris Hilton even showed up for the anniversary celebration.

Remmer's Bierstuben (beer house), Bremen, Germany, 1950s.

Just as internationally famous as Oktoberfest is Munich's Hofbräuhaus am Platzl, the world's best-known beer hall or cellar. Hofbräuhaus translates as 'court brew house' and the Bavarian state-owned institution has a history dating back to 1589, when Duke Wilhelm v decreed a brewery should be built on the site of the royal residence. In 1607 Duke Maximilian I constructed a brewery to produce weissbier on the site of the present Hofbräuhaus, which became the brewery 'tap' in 1828.

The beer hall – with its long, communal tables, local meat dishes and traditional house band – is a long-standing element of Bavarian popular culture, and the Hofbräuhaus in Munich has played a significant part in Germany's political culture, too. The official website notes Mozart and Lenin as habitués of the venue, but fails to mention that Adolf Hitler and his Nazi supporters often used the premises, along with other Munich beer halls, to proclaim policies and entertain guests. Meanwhile, what has become known as the 'Beer Hall Putsch'

Hofbräuhaus, Munich, 1905.

of 1923, when Hitler tried to seize power, took place in the
Bürgerbräukeller beer hall, which was located on the east side
of Munich.

So imprinted into the popular consciousness is the Hofbräuhaus style of Germanic beer consumption that it has
spawned a chain of branded beer halls across Germany and
beyond, with Hofbräuhaus beers even being brewed under
licence in u.s. brew-pubs. As well as the beer hall, another
notable feature of German beer drinking is the existence of
the beer garden, which has now become a popular element of
beer consumption all over the world, though it was actually
first adopted in the u.s. from the middle of the nineteenth century. The oldest surviving beer garden in New York City is the
Bohemian Hall and Beer Garden, which dates from 1919. The
world's largest beer garden is, predictably, located in Munich,
and named the Hirschgarten. It can accommodate a remarkable 8,000 customers and offers beers from several companies.

If beer gardens arrived in the U.S. along with an influx of German immigrants during the nineteenth century, the country already boasted a long tradition and evolution of drinking venues. During the colonial era from the seventeenth century onwards, drinking was centred principally on taverns, which were classless and usually quite civilized places in which to congregate and find refreshment. Women and even children were welcome, and the taverns usually provided accommodation and food in addition to alcohol. The most salubrious would be equipped with a parlour as well as a bar, and they also often played a role as informal local courthouses.

The rise of the sort of 'Wild West' saloon bar with which we are all familiar thanks to cinema began to develop with the gradual westward expansion of the American frontier during the second half of the nineteenth century. The saloon bars of frontier towns were altogether less cosmopolitan than the taverns back east, usually male-only preserves, with the

An American bar, early 20th century.

exception of ladies laid on for entertainment of various kinds. Hard drinking was the order of the day, and only the more upmarket establishments provided meals and rooms to rent. The period of Prohibition from 1920 to 1933 gave rise to a different kind of U.S. drinking establishment, the illegal 'speakeasy', drinking dens so named because people spoke about them in hushed tones so as not to give away their identities or locations. Many were linked to organized crime and drinks were usually extremely expensive. Unlike the saloons of old, however, women were frequently to be found in speakeasies, as the atmosphere tended to be fun and conspiratorial, with cocktails served to disguise the poor quality of much of the liquor on offer.

Drinking Rituals

So much for the venues where beer drinking takes place, but what of the many and varied rituals that have grown up around it?

A beer-drinking practice peculiar to the UK and Australia is the purchasing of 'rounds' of drinks – sometimes known in Australia as 'shouts' – by members of a group, with each taking his or her turn to buy everyone a drink as the drinking progresses. Failure to buy your round is a serious misdemeanour! The concept of the round of drinks is thought to date back to the legend of King Arthur and the famous, democratic round table where his knights are supposed to have assembled. The custom of buying rounds of drinks was banned in some locations in the UK during the First World War as it was said to encourage over-consumption, which was harmful to the war effort on the home front. Australia also attempted to address the issue of drunkenness in 1916, when the sale of

Edouard Manet, *At the Café, c.* 1879.

alcohol was banned after 6 p.m. This led to unedifying scenes of Australian drinkers dashing from work to bar in order to down as much as possible before time was called. Remarkably, this piece of legislation survived until the late 1960s.

While the buying of rounds persists in the UK and Australia, most other countries operate a system where an open 'tab' is kept running while drinking takes place, with the bill being settled at the end of the session. In the USA, patrons in a bar might sometimes wait to be seated together, as a couple or group, whereas Germans tend to be much more sociable about their drinking, often sitting at a long, communal table when someone has vacated a place.

While once beer drinking was almost unknown in China, with the average Chinese consuming around half a bottle of beer per year 50 years ago – less than a resident of Iran – by 2007 each Chinese adult was drinking nearly 103 beers per year, and beer etiquette has developed accordingly. The Chinese drinking practice known as *gam bei*, which means 'dry glass' or cup, is now applied to beer with enthusiasm, and if the host or group leader says *gam bei* – effectively a toast like 'cheers' – then the rest of the guests or group members must empty their glasses. Etiquette demands that if a toast is made with beer, then all the drinkers in the party must continue to drink beer. Changing to another drink such as wine would cause significant offence. While China has been getting to grips with the art of beer drinking, the Japanese have opted to embrace technology with the intention of improving the beer-drinking experience, with leading brewer Asahi heading innovations. These have included a method of rapidly chilling beer bottles from room temperature, a machine that tilts the glass to the optimum angle for the most efficient pour, and even a robot bartender.

In the cities of Peru, beer-drinking rituals with their origins in ancient Andean culture still survive among groups of young men. After an early Sunday morning football match, the group retires to a bar where the first bottle of beer, usually the local brew Cristal, is purchased by one individual, who is also supplied with one glass. He fills the glass with beer, passes the bottle to the person on his right, drinks from the glass and empties the dregs onto the floor. He then passes the glass to the person holding the bottle, and the ritual continues around the table. Emptying the glass onto the floor both cleans it for the next drinker and also reaffirms an old tradition from the Andes of paying homage to Mother Earth. The shared glass epitomizes the bond between those gathered together. Today, although this idiosyncratic way of drinking beer persists in Lima and other Peruvian centres of population, many younger drinkers are unaware of the historical and cultural significance of the ritual.

More 'mainstream' drinking rituals include the 'yard of ale', a long-standing initiation ceremony in the UK and U.S., which consists of the rapid consumption of 3 imperial pints of beer (in the UK) from a glass vessel which is 1 yard (90 cm) in length, with a bulb at one end and flared at the other. The vessel has its origins in seventeenth-century England; one plausible explanation that is offered for its origins is that it would be filled with ale and handed from the window of an inn to a stagecoach driver who was making a brief stop, allowing him to rapidly slake his thirst without dismounting from his seat.

In Germany, there is a communal aspect to a similar custom, known as *Stiefeltrinken*, which translates as 'boot drinking'. A glass boot filled with one to two litres of beer is passed from drinker to drinker, seated around a table, with each imbiber raising the boot and swigging from it before handing it on. As the beer level falls beyond the 'ankle' of the boot, air enters, spraying beer into the face of the unwary participant. The trick, apparently, is to lower the tip of the boot as soon as air enters, without removing your mouth from the rim of the boot. Whoever finally fails to prevent spillage must pay for the next boot of beer.

The pint beer glass: the quintessential vessel associated with British beer.

Drinking Vessels

Although the art of making glass was known as long ago as the seventh century BC, the mass production of glassware really only came about with the Industrial Revolution, and therefore the practice of drinking beer from glasses – or even yards or boots – is a relatively modern phenomenon, given the long history of its consumption. Of course, it may seem to the uninitiated that beer could be consumed in any vessel that does not actually leak, but that is far from the truth. The British tend to stand out from most beer-drinking crowds due to the continued use of imperial measures, with pint (1.2 U.S. pints/ 568 ml) and half-pint glasses still being de rigueur, though some bars have introduced one-third-of-a-pint glasses in recent years in an attempt to get younger and more adventurous drinkers to sample a wider range of craft beers, perhaps offering a 'flight' of three one-third pints of varying brands or styles. Such 'flights' are also popular in the u.s., but here matters become slightly confusing for the Brit abroad, as a u.s. pint is defined as 473 millitres, or 0.8 imperial pints. Traditionally, pint glasses have come in 'straight' and 'tankard'

Traditional German beer stein.

Toby jug and German souvenir-style beer tankard. Ceramic Toby jugs were first developed in Staffordshire in the 1760s. The origin of the name is disputed, but some say 'Toby' is named after Sir Toby Belch from Shakespeare's *Twelfth Night*.

format, with Scottish and Northern English drinkers often dismissing the tankard as an effete, southern vessel, and not a 'real man's' glass.

Germany has long been associated with the stein – originally made of stoneware but now of glass, and containing a litre of liquid. However, these now tend to be used principally in beer gardens and beer halls which are popular with tourists, who also frequently buy a stein as a souvenir of their visit to the German beer heartlands of Bavaria. In general, German and Belgian beer drinkers take their glassware more seriously than most imbibers, matching the glass to the style of beer being consumed. Indeed, in the German city of Cologne, kölsch – which by law can only be brewed in the Cologne region – is served at a temperature around 10°C in a long, thin, cylindrical 0.2-litre glass, known as a *stange* or 'pole'.

A Belgian bar will serve a bock, faro, gueze or lambic in a flute-style glass, which showcases colour and retains carbonation, while a stemmed goblet will be used for a dark ale, a dubbel or tripel ale, as it maintains the beer's head and offers a wide rim for deep, satisfying sips. Pilsner and witbier come in slender, tapered, 'pilsner' glasses, which showcase clarity and carbonation and preserve the beer's head. The list goes on, but the point is that pairing a beer with an appropriate glass enhances the physical drinking experience and is not

Belgian beer glasses come in a wide variety of styles.

Vincent van Gogh, *Woman in the Café Tambourin*, 1887.

just a whim or affectation. Happily for beer drinkers, more and more establishments, especially in the U.S., are catching on to the virtues of embracing style-appropriate glassware.

Beer and Food

As many people know from experience, drinking beer increases the appetite, but for centuries, beer has been seen as a 'poor man's drink', an everyday alcoholic beverage simply intended to slake the thirst. Whereas wine has a long and noble tradition as the accompaniment to good food, it is only in recent years that many nations have begun to consider beer a viable companion to fine cuisine. At the same time, whisky has also emerged as a candidate for food pairing, as a growing number of people have become receptive to combinations of less obvious food and drink types.

It is only common sense to pair beer and food, since from time immemorial beer was consumed alongside those other staples of life – bread and cheese. Beer works with everything from a packet of pork scratchings (rinds) or cheese and onion crisps (potato chips) to a seven-course gourmet banquet, and 'fine cuisine' need not mean expensive and overly fussy but rather anything with integrity and local provenance – much like the best beers themselves.

A traditional German mid-morning snack is wheat beer and sausages (weissbier and weisswurst), and countries that have traditionally taken their beer seriously have a longer history of combining it with a range of meals, most notably Belgium and Germany. Other countries are starting to catch up, however, and dedicated beer menus and even beer sommeliers are an increasingly common sight in restaurants across Britain. The art of beer and food pairing has been boosted as the diverse stylistic output of craft breweries has given much greater scope for creative cooks, chefs and menu planners. Beer actually offers a much wider potential spectrum of flavour characteristics than wine, due to the diversity of ingredients, and brewing and cooking have much more in common than wine making and cooking. Beer can range from the full-bodied, sweet, rich and malty to the bitter, heavily hopped and light-bodied, with many variations in between.

When matching beer and food there are a few, relatively commonsense points to bear in mind. One is never to overwhelm one or the other. A light-bodied, delicate summer ale would be drowned, as it were, by a very rich and fully flavoured food, just as a powerful, malty, winter ale would leave few nuances to be discovered in a subtle and mildly flavoured dish.

Chicken, fish, salads and pastas combine ideally with a light German lager, blonde or wheat ale, though a silky, smoky stout balances the creaminess of smoked salmon. Dry Irish stout and oysters is a wonderful combination instead of the more customary white wine – just head to Galway in the autumn for the International Oyster and Seafood Festival to experience this particular match made in heaven at its most authentic.

More assertively carbonated beers are ideal to counter fatty cuisine and serve to refresh the palate, while sweet, malty ales act to combat overt saltiness in a dish. For example, a

There is a style of beer to suit virtually every dish.

Cuisine de la Bière

The Belgians take their beer and food combinations so seriously that they even have a specific phrase for the concept – cuisine de la bière – which embraces both beer/food pairings and cooking with beer. Here are some suggestions for Belgian beer styles and accompanying dishes.

Blonde or golden ale	spicy chicken
Blanche or white beer	tartiflette (cheesy potato bake)
Red ale	garlic turkey sausage
Lambic beer	roast chicken with rosemary
Kriek beer	strawberry or cherry cheesecake
Gueuze beer	sels
Brown beer	steak au poivre

carbonated, fruity Belgian witbier is the perfect complement to oily fish dishes, such as salmon or sardines. Here the combination works by contrast, but sometimes pairing similar flavours works well, too. The caramel notes of an old-fashioned ale or stout style mirror those present in roast or grilled pork or beef. An India Pale Ale works nicely in combination with spicy dishes such as curries or Mexican cuisine. The roast malts found in stout make this style of beer a winner with barbecued meat, which has a note of char to it, while a British bitter beer goes well with the components of a classic ploughman's lunch.

Fully flavoured, strong beers are ideal alongside the extreme sweetness of many desserts, and stout works notably well with chocolate. Try crème brûlée and barley wine – the bittersweet notes of the beer counter the sweetness of the dessert, without providing too dramatic a contrast – but contrasts can be good with the final course of the meal, too, and cheesecake and IPA work well in opposition. A dark Belgian beer or a barley wine provides the perfect mate for fine milk chocolate.

With the cheeseboard, beer really comes into its own, and as there are so many cheeses of varying styles and character to experiment with, the potential beer–cheese permutations are almost unending. The fruity, salty character of hard cheeses made from cow's milk, such as Cheddar, Gruyère and Gouda, partner ideally with an IPA or a lively pilsner, while a less likely but highly effective variant is to opt for something which mirrors the character of the cheese, such as a barley wine, with its rich malt and fruit notes. The sweetness also contrasts nicely with the saltiness of the cheese. Wheat beers prove particularly effective when matched to soft cheeses made from cow's milk, such as Brie and Camembert, while brown ale also suits such cheeses.

To round off a meal, there is no need to reach for the cognac or single malt Scotch whisky – Belgian tripels, barrel-aged beers and anything described as 'imperial' or 'double' will provide a great accompaniment to a hand-rolled cigar, a cup of coffee and good conversation. Of course, there is no need to go for full-blown matching of a beer to each course. Feel your way into the whole concept of pairings, learn what works and what doesn't work; don't be afraid to experiment – and above all, enjoy! It is helpful to visit some of the many gastropubs and restaurants that offer food–beer pairings, both for pure pleasure and also to get ideas for your own dinner parties or less formal pairings.

7
Beer and Culture

Considering the long and important role beer has played in the lives of people all over the world, it is not surprising that imbibers have chosen to commemorate, celebrate and immortalize it in whatever cultural media have been available at the time. So it is that songs relating to beer drinking abound, as do references to it in literature, while the twentieth century saw beer taking its place in film and on television. Beer has also become a potent force in global advertising and sponsorship around the world.

Beer in Literature

Given that writing and drinking are intimate bedfellows in the popular imagination, and that there is a certain justification for this view, it is not surprising that many writers have embraced the subject of beer, both in their lives and in their art.

William Shakespeare was certainly no stranger to ale through his intimate associations with Elizabethan tavern life, and the product features in a number of his plays. In *The Winter's Tale* (*c.* 1610–11) the character Autolycus declares 'For a quart of ale is a dish for a king', while a boy in *Henry V* states:

'I would give all my fame for a pot of ale and safety.' Ale was widely sold in theatres during Shakespeare's time and was reputedly used to help douse the flames that destroyed the original Globe Theatre in London in 1613, after a spark from a cannon ignited the thatched roof during a performance of *Henry VIII*. It is appropriate, then, that the shop at the recreated Globe on London's Bankside sells three bespoke beers, namely Globe Stout, Globe Ale and Globe Blond.

Shakespeare's monarch Elizabeth I was herself a devoted toper of ale, at a time when ale was routinely drunk in preference to that altogether more dangerous liquid, water. It was said that Her Majesty could out-drink any man at court and her preferred breakfast was bread and ale. When the queen entertained Robert Dudley, the Earl of Leicester, at Hatfield House, it was recorded that the ale provided was not of sufficient strength to please Her Majesty, and 'we were fain to send to London . . . her own bere was so strong as there was no man able to drink it'.

One of the finest pieces of English literature relating to beer was penned by A. E. Housman in his verse collection *A Shropshire Lad* (1896). The final two lines are often quoted out of context and applied to Scotch whisky, but taken as a whole there can be no doubt which drink Housman had in mind:

> Say, for what were hop-yards meant,
> Or why was Burton built on Trent?
> Oh many a peer of England brews
> Livelier liquor than the Muse,
> And malt does more than Milton can
> To justify God's way to man.

Across the Irish Sea, beer, and particularly porter and stout, loom large in the nation's literature. Flann O'Brien – or

Brian O'Nolan, to give him his 'birth name' – was of the generation of Irish writer-drinkers that also included such epic topers as Brendan Behan and Patrick Kavanagh. In his surreal novel *At Swim-Two-Birds* (1939) O'Brien has a character declare in a poem titled 'The Workman's Friend',

> When things go wrong and will not come right,
> Though you do the best you can,
> When life looks black as the hour of night –
> A pint of plain is your only man.

The last line means that a pint of stout will solve all your problems.

Despite fierce competition, Brendan Behan emerges triumphant as the king of Irish drinking writers; indeed he famously described himself as 'a drinker with a writing problem'. The political activist, playwright and essayist enjoyed a glass of porter or stout as much as his contemporaries, and he enjoyed a dozen glasses even more. In *Brendan Behan's Island* (1962) he lamented the recent decline in the consumption of porter, declaring that previously 'it was so good that the glass it was in used to stick to the counter'.

James Joyce was a confirmed porter drinker, but it was a glass of burgundy that was consumed by Leopold Bloom in Joyce's epic novel *Ulysses* (1918–20), and which now features in the annual Bloomsday celebrations, replicating the fictional events of 16 June 1904 as featured in the novel. Appropriately enough, the first Bloomsday was held in 1954 to commemorate the 50th anniversary of the events of the book, and Flann O'Brien and Patrick Kavanagh were central to the pilgrimage along the '*Ulysses* route' through Dublin, though the journey was abandoned around the halfway point due to the inebriation of many of the participants.

The Welsh poet Dylan Thomas was a fellow Celt with a fondness for beer, and had a penchant for lining up a series of glasses of light ale on the bar and downing them in quick succession as a hangover cure. In his best-known work, the play *Under Milk Wood* (1954), the character Cherry Owen enjoys a regular nightly consumption of 'seventeen pints of flat, warm, thin, Welsh, bitter beer'. Thomas wrote in a letter to his wife Caitlin, 'If I touched anything else but beer I just couldn't get along'; shortly before his death in New York he reputedly returned to the Hotel Chelsea where he was staying and declared: 'I've had eighteen straight whiskies. I think that's the record!' Perhaps he should have stuck to beer, after all.

Although often associated with Scotland's national drink, whisky, and an articulate advocate of its merits, Robert Burns also wrote about, and drank, ale. In his 1789 song 'Willie Brew'd a Peck o' Maut' the poet writes of the joys of convivial consumption of ale:

> O, Willie brew'd a peck o' maut,
> And Rob and Alan cam to see;
> Three blyther hearts, that lee-lang night,
> Ye wadna found in Christendie.
> We are na fou, we're nae that fou,
> But just a drappie in our ee;
> The cock may craw, the day may daw
> And aye we'll taste the barley bree.
>
> (Oh, Willie brewed a peck of malt beer
> And Rob and Alan came to see;
> Three happier hearts the live-long night
> You would not find in Christendom.
> 'We are not drunk, we're not that drunk,
> But just slightly inebriated;

The cock may crow, the day may dawn
And always we'll drink the barley brew.')

Meanwhile, the eponymous hero of the epic poem 'Tam O' Shanter' (1790) is an Ayrshire farmer who spent a lengthy market-day evening in an Ayr tavern in the company of his drinking companion, the cobbler Souter Johnnie. The pair were 'bousing [drinking] at the nappy [strong ale], / And getting fou [drunk] and unco happy [somewhat merry]'.

Across the Atlantic, authors have celebrated beer with just as much enthusiasm as their British and Irish counterparts. Edgar Allan Poe wrote a fine short poem on the subject in July 1848, 'Lines on Ale':

Fill with mingled cream and amber,
I will drain that glass again.
Such hilarious visions clamber
Through the chambers of my brain.
Quantist thoughts – queerest fancies,
Come to life and fade away:
What care I how time advances?
I am drinking ale today.

A century later, Charles Bukowski was to drinking and writing in the USA what Brendan Behan was to the twin occupations in Ireland. A drinker of heroic proportions, beer inevitably features in many of his novels and poems. The collection of poems entitled *Love is a Dog from Hell* (1974–7) contains a piece simply titled 'Beer', which begins

I don't know how many bottles of beer
I have consumed while waiting for things
to get better

I don't know how much wine and whisky
and beer
mostly beer
I have consumed after
splits with women . . .

The movie *Barfly* (dir. Barbet Schroeder, 1987), starring Mickey
Rourke, is a fictionalized celebration of Bukowski's drinking life.

Beer in Film

If writers have a popular reputation as drinkers, then actors
surely come a close second. Think of Richard Burton, Peter
O'Toole and Richard Harris, to name but one famous trio.
As with literature, beer has featured in many great films,
and plays a somewhat controversial role in the James Bond
movie *Skyfall* (dir. Sam Mendes, 2012), in which 007 swaps his
customary martini for a glass of Heineken (see 'Beer and
Sponsorship', further on). Perhaps the best-known 'classic'
film with a beer theme is *Ice Cold in Alex* (dir. J. Lee Thompson,
1958), which stars John Mills as the senior officer in charge of
an ambulance crew crossing the North African desert during
the Second World War. Captain Anson (played by Mills) is
fond of a drink and dreams of sinking a cold beer when the
group reaches Alexandria.

In the final scene Anson's dream finally becomes reality,
and genuine lager had to be used during filming of the scene
at Elstree Studios in order to obtain the authentic appearance,
requiring John Mills to down several glasses during takes.
Carlsberg was the chosen brand of lager, which was acceptable because it was brewed in Denmark: Mills and his associates
could not have been seen drinking a German lager in a war

film, and the brand specified in the novel on which the film was based was called Rheingold, which sounded altogether too Teutonic.

Less 'classic' but also a movie with plenty of action, *Smokey and the Bandit* (dir. Hal Needham, 1977), starring Burt Reynolds, has beer at the very core of its plot. Bo 'Bandit' Darville (Reynolds) is recruited by Big Enos Burdette to drive a trailer loaded with 400 cases of Coors beer from Texarkana, Texas, to Georgia – a journey of 1,800 miles undertaken in 28 hours while evading the highway patrol, known as 'smokeys'. The premise is that Coors was only distributed in a limited number of states west of the Mississippi River at that time, and numerous truckers attempting to run Coors into Georgia had previously been arrested. Essentially, the movie takes the form of a protracted car chase, and there is a degree of artistic licence in the distance to be covered, which in reality is considerably less than 1,800 miles, while Texarkana is situated in a 'dry' county!

The film *Beer* (dir. Patrick Kelly, 1985) could hardly advertise its subject-matter more overtly, and the comedy is a satire of the advertising industry, with ad executive B. D. Tucker (played by Loretta Swit) concerned that she will lose the account of Norbecker Brewery. In an attempt to keep the account she elicits the support of three 'average Joes' who inadvertently foil a bar robbery, building an ad campaign around them. The adverts are a success, but to keep Norbecker Beer happy, Tucker has to create ever more sexist and offensive adverts, even devising the slogan 'Whip Out Your Norbecker'.

Finally, beer fact rather than beer fiction, *American Beer* appeared in 2002, a documentary directed by Paul Kermizian about five friends from New York City who set out to visit 38 breweries in 40 days. The resulting film was described by its makers as a 'bockumentary'.

Beer in Music

The earliest songs relating to beer and its consumption tended to take the form of ballads, with the Tudor comic drama 'Gammer Gurton's Needle', written around 1553, containing the lines 'No frost or snow, no wind I trow, / Can hurt me if I wold; / I am so wrapped, and thoroughly lapped / Of jolly good ale and old'.

The best-known beer ballad is 'John Barleycorn', in which the eponymous character is the personification of the barley crop and the beer and whisky which may be created from it. In the ballad, John Barleycorn suffers attacks and ultimately death, corresponding to the various stages of barley cultivation, such as reaping and malting. Ultimately, Barleycorn may die, but in doing so he provides life-enhancing alcohol for the enjoyment of others.

The most popular version of 'John Barleycorn' was penned by Robert Burns in 1782, but there are several earlier variants, and one such English version begins with the lines

> There was three men come out o' the west
> their fortunes for to try,
> And these three men made a solemn vow,
> John Barleycorn must die,
> They ploughed, they sowed, they harrowed him in,
> throwed clods upon his head,
> And these three men made a solemn vow,
> John Barleycorn was dead.

Of more modern beer-drinking songs, the most popular is probably 'The Drinking Song' from the Broadway operetta *The Student Prince* (1924) filmed in 1954 with Edmund Purdom playing the role of Prince Karl Franz, though Mario Lanza

Cover for the sheet music of the song 'Bitter Beer' with a portrait of the singer, T. Maclagan, 1864.

dubbed all of the songs. The film features an inn popular with Heidelberg university students, where 'The Drinking Song' is performed. It opens with the lines 'Ein zwei drei vier / Lift your stein and drink your beer.' When the play was first performed on Broadway during the 1920s, this song was particularly enthusiastically received by thirsty Prohibition-era audiences.

Inevitably, popular music genres have featured beer, notably blues and country, and the songs in question do not always relate to a macho beer culture. Tennessee-born bluesman Memphis Slim recorded 'Beer Drinking Woman', which, as stated in the introduction to the song, set in Rubin's Tavern, Chicago, during 1940. It tells the story of how he had $45 when he entered a beer tavern 'to give a girl a nice time', but left with only a dime.

Country music embraces legendary drinking performers such as George Jones, though his personal preference during his drinking days was for hard liquor, but he did record 'Beer Run', which celebrates driving in a truck at 90 mph to the county line to buy beer.

There is even a double CD entitled *Best Ever Country Drinking Songs* (Australia similarly boasts a double-CD set, *Australia's Best Beer Ballads*) which includes Tom T. Hall's 'I Like Beer' and possibly the finest country beer song, Glenn Sutton's 'What Made Milwaukee Famous?'

On the wilder side of the rock scene, Frank Zappa included the song 'Titties and Beer' on his album *Zappa in New York* (1978). It was Zappa who also came up with the oft-quoted lines 'You can't be a real country unless you have a beer and an airline – it helps if you have some kind of football team, or some nuclear weapons, but at the very least you need a beer.'

Inevitably, Germany's musical heritage features beer-related songs ancient and modern, many of which are performed at the annual Munich Oktoberfest. One available recording is *20 German Drinking Songs*, performed by The Oktoberfest Oompah Band, not to mention *German Beer Drinking Music*, which runs to a remarkable ten CDs!

Beer and World Leaders

Many of our greatest politicians and statesmen and -women have recognized the valuable contribution beer has made to life, with Queen Victoria, known to add whisky to her claret, declaring, 'Give my people plenty of beer, good beer, and cheap beer, and you will have no revolution among them.' Meanwhile, in Germany, her grandson Kaiser Wilhelm II once stated, 'Give me a woman who loves beer and I will conquer the world.' Perhaps he found her, for he certainly set out on to try. President Benjamin Franklin believed that 'beer is proof that God loves us and wants us to be happy', while his predecessor in the office, Abraham Lincoln, opined: 'I am a firm believer in the people. If given the truth, they can be depended upon to meet any national crisis. The great point is to bring them the real facts, and beer.'

Beer and Advertising

Although we tend to think of advertising today in terms of print and television commercials and online media, taverns and inns actually advertised their wares centuries ago by hanging out a piece of greenery in front of the pub to indicate that ale was available. From actual greenery, this in time became a sign – a graphic depiction of a bush, similarly designed to inform the illiterate that ale was available on the premises. From those medieval beginnings evolved the naming of taverns and the business of illustrating those names on signage.

Many of the pub names still common across Britain today have ancient origins. For example, although a pub called The Bull may seem to have simple associations with agriculture, it could actually denote the Catholic allegiance of a long-past

The popular British pub name 'Golden Lion' has heraldic origins.

innkeeper, since during the Reformation in the time of Henry VIII (1491–1547) a papal bull – or proclamation – threatened Henry with excommunication after he rejected the Catholic faith following the 1533 annulment of the monarch's marriage to Catherine of Aragon. The naming of an inn The Bull was possibly a sign of solidarity with Rome. From a similar source comes a possible explanation of the popular pub name The Cat and Fiddle. One plausible theory as to the origin of the name is that it is a corruption of Catherine la Fidèle – Catherine the Faithful – a sobriquet often applied to Catherine of Aragon, first wife of Henry VIII and to Catholics the true queen of England. As with The Bull, naming your tavern The Cat and Fiddle could be interpreted as a sign of support for Catherine and the Catholic Church.

The Turk's Head and Saracen's Head probably have their origins in gruesome trophies brought back by Christian knights from the Middle East during the numerous Crusades against the Muslims conducted between 1095 and 1291, though it is also possible that inns close to the sea bearing the Turk's Head name actually refer to a knot used when constructing nets by fishermen on the south and west coasts. The knot is so named because of its likeness to a turban.

The Three Horseshoes may have originally denoted an inn close to the forge of a blacksmith, indicating that a lost horseshoe – they usually have four, after all – could be replaced there. Horseshoes also denote good luck, perhaps because fairies were thought to be afraid of iron for some reason, and an iron horseshoe was easy to come by and hang above a door to keep the fairies at bay. The Chequers probably took its name from the fact that the chequerboard was a widely used symbol of money-lenders, and where better for them to carry out their trade than a tavern? Some pub names are rather more obvious in their derivations. For example, a pub called The Cock almost certainly took its title from the fact that cockfighting took place on the premises in cockpits, before the sport was banned in England and Wales in 1835.

So it was that taverns indicated their individuality, but the advertising of specific brands of beer did not really gain momentum until the mid-nineteenth century; with advances in print technology it became possible to produce eye-catching, colourful posters, which were widely used in both Europe and the USA. In the UK, John Gilroy produced some of the most memorable print adverts for any product with his commissions for Guinness, featuring a toucan and the strapline 'Guinness is good for you', no longer viable in these times of the Trade Descriptions Act and increased sensitivity to the effects of over-indulgence in alcohol. Nonetheless, Guinness remains one of the most creative of all beer advertisers.

Just as it is no longer acceptable to claim that beer is good for you, so the term 'milk stout' has also fallen by the wayside, since the stout in question does not actually contain milk but is brewed with an amount of milk sugar, or lactose. This did not prevent Mackeson – probably the best-known purveyors of the drink – displaying a milk churn on the label when it introduced its milk stout in 1907, while several rival versions featured cows. Mackeson went on to use a strapline which echoed the apparently positive health effects of beer suggested by Guinness: 'It looks good, tastes good and by golly it does you good.'

In a promotional poster for Budweiser in the USA Adolphus Busch famously took an existing painting titled *Custer's Last Fight* in 1896 and had some extra Indian scalpings added to heighten the effect. Budweiser's great rival Miller managed to alter the perception of its Miller Lite from that of a low-calorie beer aimed at diet-conscious women to a beer which could be drunk by men in large quantities. The slogan that accompanied the astonishingly successful 1970s print and TV campaign was 'Tastes great, less filling', and after volumes of Miller Lite doubled during the 1970s the brand overtook Budweiser as the best-selling American beer in 1992.

Across the Canadian border, Molson achieved cult status with its cinema and television advertising campaign for Molson Canadian featuring what was known as 'Joe's Rant'. It was a controversial assertion of Canadian identity, voiced by a figure wearing a plaid shirt against a backdrop of Canadian icons. The lengthy 'rant' opens with the lines 'Hey! I'm not a lumberjack or a fur trader and I don't live in an igloo or eat blubber, or own a dogsled', culminating with 'Canada is the second-largest landmass! The first nation of hockey! And the best part of North America! My name is Joe! And I am *Canadian*! Thank you.' Such was the success of this advert that people in bars asked for the volume to be turned up when it aired, while at sporting events word-perfect fans chanted along to it.

In Europe, a number of brewers have used quirky and original advertising ploys, with Heineken gaining a great deal of mileage from its long-term slogan 'Refreshes the parts other beers cannot reach', while Carlsberg's equally famous tagline 'Probably the best lager in the world' was created in 1973 by leading UK advertising agency Saatchi & Saatchi, with the original advert voiced by Orson Welles.

Stella Artois, meanwhile, took the gamble of suggesting its product was costly, implying that the reason for this was its high quality. The brand adopted the phrase 'Reassuringly expensive' and produced a series of UK television campaigns which imitated the style of European cinema, commencing with a number of adverts based on the French film *Jean de Florette* (1986). If the intention of Stella Artois was to associate the brand with sophisticated European tastes, then Foster's lager adverts from the 1970s to the present day have adopted an almost polar opposite approach in relation to Australian culture. Slogans such as 'The amber nectar' and 'Australian for beer' were allied with caricatures of Australian stereotypes, including visuals such as kangaroos and hats with corks hanging from them. The actor Barry Humphries and his crude Bazza McKenzie character made the brand an almost overnight sensation in the UK during the 1970s, while the following decade saw the star of the hit movie *Crocodile Dundee* (1986), Paul Hogan, continue the beer's high-profile commercial success as the face of Foster's, playing the role of a plain-speaking Australian in London.

Advertising for Heineken, Bucharest, Romania.

Humour has always been at the core of Foster's campaigns, and the success of Foster's in Britain led fellow Australian brand Castlemaine xxxx to develop its own series of light-hearted UK television adverts, focusing on apparently archetypal aspects of Australian character. As with Carlsberg some years earlier, the Castlemaine account was in the hands of Saatchi & Saatchi, who used humour and innuendo, adopting the phrase 'Australians wouldn't give a Castlemaine xxxx for anything else.' One of the most popular and successful examples of Castlemaine xxxx advertising featured a group of sheep-shearers loading their battered pickup truck with many cases of xxxx in preparation for an outing. When two bottles of sweet sherry, 'for the ladies', are added to the load, the suspension of the pickup duly collapses. 'Looks like we've overdone it with the sherry' is the deadpan comment from one member of the party.

Beer and Sponsorship

Effective sponsorship depends on linking products to appropriate activities, so it is no great surprise to see beer sponsorships historically focusing on working-class or 'blue-collar' sports such as football (soccer), baseball, hockey and motor racing.

Given the scale of its sales and the promotional budget at its disposal, it is perhaps inevitable that Budweiser leads the way in the USA, and the brand is the official beer sponsor of Major League Baseball and sponsor of 23 out of 30 participating clubs. According to the leading American sportswriter Peter Richmond, 'there is only one game at the heart of America and that is baseball, and only one beverage to be found sloshing at the depths of our national soul and that is beer . . . Beer needs baseball, and baseball needs beer – it has always been thus.'

The Miller Lite-sponsored Dodge of Kurt Busch.

Budweiser also has a long-standing partnership with the U.S. Olympic Committee, spanning almost three decades and including fourteen Olympic Games and Winter Olympic Games. Additionally, Budweiser enjoys a partnership with the Fédération Internationale de Football Association (FIFA) and is the official beer of the 2014 FIFA World Cup, while in the UK Budweiser now sponsors the FA Cup. The brand has been involved in football-related activities for 25 years, and in 2010 sales grew by more than 36 per cent, with much of this increase being attributed to its FIFA World Cup sponsorship.

Back in the States, Budweiser's great rival MillerCoors enjoys an ongoing relationship with NASCAR racing, with Miller Lite sponsorship of a Dodge racing car and a role as the sport's official beer, as well as a number of individual track sponsorships. According to Jackie Woodward, vice president of media and marketing services at MillerCoors, 'This is an important place to be. NASCAR fans are beer drinkers. We need to be there and we need to be there for the long haul.' MillerCoors also has a major corporate sponsorship deal with the National Hockey League, replacing Budweiser brewer Anheuser-Busch in 2011.

In the UK, Carling is the official sponsor of the England football team, while Heineken replaced Amstel as the UEFA Champions League beer sponsor and is also involved in supporting the UEFA Super Cup. Meanwhile, the world of British horseracing has a long association with beer sponsorship, and Whitbread was the first commercial sponsor in British sport with its support of the Whitbread Gold Cup from 1957 until 2001.

The Mackeson Gold Cup was established in 1960, and was run as such until 1995, by which time Mackeson Stout no longer projected the required image and the sponsorship was dropped, though fellow stout brand Murphy's backed the

National Hunt event from 1996 to 1999. Today, the Heineken-owned John Smith's brand is associated with more than 90 days of flat and National Hunt racing each year, and John Smith's has been the title sponsor of the Grand National at Aintree since 2005.

Less obviously, the AB InBev-owned, Bremen-brewed Beck's brand has had a lengthy commitment to supporting artistic ventures, and currently sponsors the Green Box Project, described as 'a global fund established to inspire, celebrate and financially support independent talent in art, design, music and fashion'. In total, 1,000 individual projects are being funded and showcased and, according to Beck's, 'the resulting art pieces will be experienced via augmented-reality in Green Boxes located around the world and will be permanently displayed in the fund's virtual gallery.'

Meanwhile, fellow AB InBev brand Stella Artois has been associated with the support of film-related activities in the UK since 1994, with high-profile sponsorships at the Cannes, Melbourne and Sundance film festivals.

Staying with film and sponsorship, as briefly mentioned earlier, Heineken signed a $45 million deal with the makers of *Skyfall* that saw 007 drinking the Dutch lager, while Bond actor Daniel Craig participated in a series of television adverts for Heineken. Additionally, his image was printed on limited edition bottles ahead of the film's premiere in the USA, where Heineken hoped to raise its profile as a result of its association with the Bond franchise.

Recipes

Cooking with Beer

The smarter cooks and chefs have long known that beer is an invaluable aid to the culinary art. The carbonation of beer gives lightness to bread, cakes and heavy puddings, adding moistness and extending their shelf life. Pale ale is ideal to lighten batter. Stronger and more full-flavoured beers may be used to add body to a soup or additional colour to a sauce. Beer can also be used instead of stock, in which case, opt for something like a sweet stout. Beer has excellent tenderizing properties and when employed as a marinade is less assertive than red wine and does not mask or dominate the flavours of the food in question. After the alcohol has evaporated, what remains are the simple and natural flavours of barley and hops, which complement almost any foodstuff being marinated. Ideally, select an amber or brown ale for marinades, while witbier is perfect for poaching or steaming, especially a dish such as mussels, though it works just as well with hotdogs. When used in a glaze or baste, beer enhances the flavour of poultry and pork dishes. Beer should not be ignored when it comes to desserts, either. Try a Belgian fruit beer in fruit compote or even serve ice cream in imperial stout as a 'float'.

The best beers with which to cook are relatively low in bitterness, ideally with a sweet, malty character, and the aim should always be to opt for a light touch. The beer ought to enhance and promote the inherent flavours in the food, rather than dominate them.

Beer Recipes

Beer Brats

2 teaspoons olive oil or butter
8 bratwurst sausages
1 large onion, sliced into rings
6 fl. oz (180 ml) beer (darker beers will provide a richer flavour)

Heat 1 teaspoon of olive oil or butter. Brown sausages until deep golden brown. Remove to a plate.

To the dripping, add the remaining teaspoon of olive oil or butter and the onions. Turn the onions to coat with oil. Cook, stirring frequently, until onions are golden in colour.

Return the sausages to the pan with the onions and add the beer. Cook over medium heat, turning midway through, until beer has cooked down to a syrup, around 12–15 minutes.
Serves 4

Beer Bread

12 fl. oz (350 ml) light-bodied beer
3 cups (420 g) self-raising flour
1 teaspoon salt
⅓ cup (60 g) golden caster sugar
2 tablespoons melted butter

Mix beer, flour, salt and sugar in a bowl. Bake for 50 minutes in greased loaf tin in preheated oven at 375°F (190°C). Remove from oven 3–4 minutes before baking is complete, glaze the top of the loaf with the melted butter and return to the oven.

Carbonnade à la Flamande

3½ lb (1.6 kg) chuck roast, cut into small pieces
salt and black pepper
4 tablespoons butter
3 onions, sliced ¼ in. (0.5 cm) thick
3 tablespoons plain flour
1½ cups (340 ml) chicken or beef stock
12 fl. oz (350 ml) dark Belgian abbey ale or brown ale
4 sprigs thyme
2 bay leaves
1 tablespoon wholegrain mustard
1 tablespoon brown sugar

Season beef with salt and pepper. Heat 2 tablespoons of butter on the stove until hot. Brown the meat, without stirring, for approximately 3 minutes on each side. Transfer browned beef to a bowl.

On the stove, add 2 tablespoons butter, reduce heat to medium. Add the onions and half a teaspoon of salt; cook until onions are browned, around 15 minutes. Add flour and stir until onions are evenly coated, about 2 minutes. Stir in stock and beer, thyme, bay, browned beef and salt and pepper. Increase heat to medium to high and bring to a full simmer. Reduce heat to low, partially cover and cook for 2–3 hours until beef is tender, stirring occasionally. Add brown sugar and mustard 30 minutes before cooking is completed. Remove bay leaf and thyme, adding more salt and pepper to taste before serving.

Serves 6–8

Cheddar Cheese and Beer Soup

½ cup (125 g) onion, finely diced
1 tablespoon minced garlic
6 slices bacon, diced
1 tablespoon butter
¼ cup (35 g) plain flour

6 cups (1.35 l) vegetable stock
4–6 fl. oz (100–180 ml) pale ale
½ cup (120 ml) heavy (double) cream
2 tablespoons Worcestershire sauce
2 teaspoons horseradish sauce
2 tablespoons Dijon mustard
2 bay leaves
salt and pepper to taste
½ lb (225 g) Cheddar cheese, grated

Heat a pan over a medium heat and add the diced bacon. Cook until bacon is almost ready. Add the onion and garlic and cook for a further 3 minutes. Add butter and flour and mix thoroughly. Add vegetable stock and cook until relatively thick. Add remaining ingredients and simmer for 20 minutes. Remove bay leaves and serve with croutons.

Serves 6–8

Steak and Ale Pie

Filling
1 chopped onion
1 chopped celery stick
2 tablespoons plain flour
2 tablespoons butter
700 g stewing steak – cut into chunks
2 beef stock cubes
1 tablespoon Worcestershire sauce
1 sprig thyme
1 bottle (or ½ pint) dark ale

Pastry
1 beaten egg
500 g plain flour
250 g suet
6–8 tablespoons water

Preheat oven to 160ºC. Place celery and onion in a casserole dish and sauté with butter until soft. Stir in flour, beef and Worcestershire sauce. Add crumbled stock cubes and thyme. Pour in ale, simmer and then cook in covered dish for 2 hours 30 minutes. Remove the lid and cook uncovered for a further 30 minutes. Increase oven temperature to 200ºC.

Using a food processor mix the flour, suet and 1 teaspoon salt then progressively add water by the tablespoon while still using the processor until the ingredients come together to form a dough, approximately 6–8 tablespoons, then complete the process by hand on a floured surface. Roll out the pastry and divide into two pieces, lining a greased 20-cm pie dish with one piece. Add meat by the spoonful and pour sauce over the meat until it is covered. Use the rest of the pastry to form a crust, trim and crimp edges to seal, make a central incision in the pastry then brush it with beaten egg to glaze. Bake for a further 40 minutes.

Serves 4–6

Stout-glazed Haddock

4 haddock fillets (skinless)
2 bottles dry stout
4 large carrots, cut into sticks
1 tablespoon lemon juice
⅓ cup (115 g) honey
½ teaspoon hot sauce
olive oil
salt and pepper

Place stout and honey in a skillet and bring to the boil. Simmer at moderate heat for 20 minutes until the liquid has reduced to half a cup (slightly over 100 ml). Mix in a bowl with lemon juice, hot sauce and half a teaspoon of salt. Allow to cool. Cover the haddock with half the stout glaze in a baking dish and coat on both sides. Boil the carrots in a pan for five minutes, then drain. Place the rest of the stout glaze in the pan and boil at a high heat for 2 minutes until it thickens. Add carrots and simmer for 1 minute. Place the haddock on a baking tray, brush with olive oil and sprinkle with pepper. Broil close to the heat for 4 minutes, until cooked. Serve with the stout-glazed carrots.

Serves 4

Chocolate Beer Cake

1 cup (225 ml) wheat beer
2 cups (280 g) plain flour
2 cups (400 g) caster sugar
2 eggs
¾ cup (180 ml) sour cream
1 tablespoon baking soda (bicarbonate of soda)
1 tablespoon vanilla extract
½ cup (115 g) unsalted butter
¾ cup (105 g) cocoa powder

Whisk the sour cream, vanilla and eggs in a bowl. Pour 1 cup of beer into a saucepan and heat at medium temperature. Dice the butter and add to the beer, stirring as it melts. Then whisk in the sugar and cocoa powder, before adding the cream, vanilla and egg mixture. Whisk together, then add flour and baking soda, and mix thoroughly. Bake in a preheated oven at 350°F (180°C) for 50 minutes.

Serves 4–6

Shepherd's Pie with Stout

1 cup (225 ml) Irish stout
2 tablespoons unsalted butter
1½ lb (700 g) ground sirloin steak
1 large onion, finely chopped
2 medium-sized carrots, finely chopped
4 oz (115 g) mushrooms, finely chopped

5 tablespoons plain flour
⅓ cup (60 ml) double cream
1 tablespoon tomato purée
1½ cup (340 ml) chicken stock
2 tablespoons soy sauce
1 cup (150 g) frozen peas
table salt
black pepper

For the potato topping
2½ lb (1.2 kg) potatoes, peeled and cut into small pieces
⅓ cup (80 ml) warm double cream
1 beaten egg
2 tablespoons melted unsalted butter

Preheat oven to 375°F (190°C). Place potatoes in pan of cold water, cover and bring to the boil. Then lower heat and cook for approximately 25 minutes. Drain, then return potatoes to warm, covered pan. Melt the butter in a large skillet then add mushrooms, carrots, onions and a little salt. Cook for approximately five minutes until browning occurs. Remove from pan and replace with the steak, adding 1 teaspoon of salt and half a teaspoon of black pepper. Cook until browned, stirring regularly with spatula. Drain fat from the beef and return cooked vegetables to the pan. Add flour and tomato purée, stirring into the steak and vegetables. Cook on a medium heat for a further 3 minutes. Slowly add stout and chicken stock, lower heat and cook until the mixture thickens. Add peas and soy sauce and stir thoroughly.

Warm double cream and 2 tablespoons of butter, add to cooked potatoes and mash thoroughly. Season with salt and black pepper, then spread potatoes over the gravy in the skillet and brush with beaten egg. Cook for 35 minutes at 380°F (195°C), until potatoes are browned.

Serves 4–6

Belgian Bacon Waffles with Chocolate Oatmeal Stout

1 cup (225 ml) chocolate oatmeal stout
2 cups (140 g) oat flour
2 eggs
3 teaspoons baking powder
½ teaspoon salt
1 teaspoon orange peel
¼ cup (55 ml) oil
1 teaspoon vanilla extract
½ cup (100 g) crisp-cooked and crumbled bacon
butter
maple syrup

Preheat and grease waffle iron. Combine flour, baking powder, salt and orange peel in a mixing bowl. Add eggs, beer, oil and vanilla extract and whisk, then fold in the bacon. Pour the batter into the waffle iron and cook until brown. Serve with maple syrup and a drizzle of melted butter.
Serves 4–6

Mussels Steamed in Belgian Golden Ale

3 lb (1.4 kg) cleaned mussels
2 sliced leeks
1 cup (25 g) chopped parsley
5 cloves chopped garlic
½ cup (120 ml) crème fraîche
2 tablespoons stoneground mustard
1½ cups (340 ml) Belgian golden ale
2 tablespoons unsalted butter
juice of 2 lemons

Chop leeks, garlic and parsley, then mix the crème fraîche with the mustard in a bowl. Warm a large pan on high heat and add the butter. Heat until it browns then add leeks and garlic. Allow to brown for approximately 4 minutes, then add the mussels and stir thoroughly. Add crème fraîche and mustard mixture and stir in, then cover the pot. Steam for 3 minutes then add the parsley and the lemon juice. Stir again, and steam for a further 2 minutes, until the mussels open.

Serves 4–6

Dill Pickle Dip with Geuze

8 oz (225 g) cream cheese
1 cup (240 ml) sour cream
6 finely chopped dill pickle spears
$\frac{1}{3}$ cup (75 ml) geuze
2 tablespoons pickle juice
2 tablespoons dill mustard
2 teaspoons dried dill
$\frac{1}{2}$ teaspoon salt

Place all the ingredients in a food mixer bowl and agitate until a creamy consistency is achieved. Cover and chill for at least two hours before serving.

IPA Cherry Tart

$\frac{1}{2}$ cup (120 ml) IPA
1 sheet puff pastry
3 cups (600 g) sweet cherries
2 tablespoons cornflour
$\frac{2}{3}$ cup (125 g) caster sugar
1 lightly beaten egg

Roll out puff pastry and place in a greased pan with removable base. Boil the IPA, sugar, cherries and cornflour in a pan on a high heat for 10 minutes until thickened, stirring regularly. Prick pastry thoroughly with a fork and glaze with beaten egg. Pour in the cherry mixture and bake at 375°F (190°C) for 20 minutes, until pastry has browned.

Beer Cocktails

We associate cocktails with spirits rather than beer, but historically beer has often been mixed with other drinks, creating, for example, shandy (beer and lemonade) and snakebite (beer and cider). However, the past few years have seen a developing trend for more cutting-edge beer-based mixed drinks, originating from that locus of beer innovation, Portland, Oregon. As with all successful trends, internationalism beckons, and today beer cocktails are being served in hip bars from Tokyo to Toronto, Los Angeles to London. Here are some popular alternatives to a highball or a whiskey sour, starting with an old classic.

Beer Margarita

12 fl. oz (350 ml) light-bodied, light-flavoured beer
12 fl. oz (350 ml) can frozen limeade concentrate
12 fl. oz (350 ml) tequila
12 fl. oz (350 ml) water
1 lime
Salt

Mix together beer, tequila, limeade and water in a jug. Add ice and garnish with wedges of lime. Serve in glasses rimmed with salt.
Serves 6

Black and Tan

½ pint stout
½ pint pale ale
54

Carefully pour the pale ale into a pint glass then add the stout by pouring it over a spoon. The stout will remain above the pale ale, hence the name.

Breakfast Beer Cocktail No. 2
—Created by Trevor Kallies, beverage director of Donnelly Group, Vancouver, Canada

1 fl. oz (30 ml) Tanqueray gin
1 fl. oz (30 ml) Cointreau
1½ teaspoons Orgeat (almond syrup)
2 dashes orange bitters
2 fl. oz (50 ml) Kronenbourg blanc

Pour the Tanqueray and Cointreau into a cocktail mixing glass. Add Orgeat, orange bitters and beer. Add ice, then shake and strain into a martini glass for serving.

Black Velvet

chilled stout
chilled brut champagne

Pour the stout into a champagne flute until it is half full. Slowly add the champagne to fill the glass.

Cucumber Blonde Bloody Mary
—created by mixologist David Nepove

2 fl. oz (50 ml) Effen cucumber vodka
4 cherry (grape) tomatoes
1 dash celery salt
1 dash pepper
2 dashes Worcestershire sauce
1 dash hot sauce
1 tablespoon lime juice
2 fl. oz (50 ml) blonde beer
celery stick, to garnish

Mix tomatoes, celery salt and pepper in a cocktail shaker. Add all other ingredients, except the beer. Add ice and shake, then strain into a glass filled with ice. Add the beer and garnish with a celery stick.

Appendix: Great Beer Brands

Amstel, The Netherlands

The Amstel brand of Dutch pilsner has been owned by Heineken since 1968, and production now takes place in the Heineken brewery at Zoeterwoude. The original Amstel brewery was established in Amsterdam during 1870 and named after the Amstel river, ice from which was used for purposes of refrigeration. Exports to the UK commenced as early as 1883, and today Amstel sells in more than 90 countries worldwide. It is the third-largest beer brand in Europe. Much is made in promotional material of the fact that the beer is 'slow-brewed' to give it a unique character.

Anchor Steam Beer, USA

Anchor Steam Beer is brewed by San Francisco's Anchor Brewing Company and has its origins in 1896. 'Steam' beers were once common in the western states of the USA, and were intended to be attractive to eastern U.S. palates familiar with a lager-drinking tradition. The term 'steam' may derive from the fact that barrels were highly pressurized and released a cloud of what appeared to be steam when they were tapped. The Anchor Brewing Company was rescued from serious financial difficulties by Fritz Maytag in 1965, and Steam Beer – a refreshing amber ale – was first bottled six years later.

Asahi, Japan

The Osaka Beer Brewing Company was established in 1889, launching Asahi beers three years later. Clearly demonstrating that beer halls are not exclusive to Germany, the company opened its first in 1897, and can claim other notable 'firsts', including Japan's earliest bottled beer (1900) and earliest canned beer (1958). Asahi – Japanese for 'rising sun' – offers a range of products including Asahi Black, a 'black' lager, Asahi Stout and Super Dry, which appeared in 1987 and was designed specifically to complement food. It has enjoyed great success, both at home and overseas, and is the leading imported Japanese beer in the UK.

Baltika, Russia

Baltika Breweries was formed in 2006 by the merger of Baltika and three other Russian breweries, and two years later the Carlsberg Group acquired a majority interest in the business. Baltika is the largest Russian brewing company and was originally founded in 1978, when the country was under Soviet rule, with the large-scale Baltika brewery in St Petersburg opening in 1990. The Baltika brand name has only been used since 1992, and the current portfolio includes Baltika No. 2 Pale, Baltika No. 3 Classic and Baltika No. 4 Classic, along with porter, export and wheat beers. Baltika boasts more than 37 per cent of the total Russian beer market, and operates twelve breweries.

Becks, Germany

One of the flagship brews of owner AB InBev, Beck's is brewed in the city of Bremen, Germany, and is the best-selling German beer brand in the world, being available in some 90 countries. Beck's was locally owned until 2002, when it was sold to what was then Interbrew for €1.8 million. The brewery had been established in 1873 by Lüder Rutenberg, Heinrich Beck and Thomas

May under the name Kaiserbrauerei Beck & May o.H.G. and the export market was targeted from the start. Stylistically, Beck's Pilsner is crisp, with hops balanced by sweet, mellow notes and good carbonation.

Bernard, Czech Republic

Although the Bernard brewing operation has only existed in its present form for just over two decades, the actual brewery, located in Humpolec, was founded during the sixteenth century. In October 1991 Stanislav Bernard, Josef Vávra and Rudolf Šmejkal were the highest bidders in an auction for the bankrupt brewing business and have gone on to create a highly regarded range of traditional beers, headed by Celebration, Amber and Dark lagers. Bernard has its own farm-based floor maltings in Rajhrad, by Brno, and produces beers that are 'micro-filtered' rather than pasteurized. Since 2001 the Belgian brewing company Duvel Moortgat has been a partner in the Bernard business.

Brains SA, Wales

S. A. Brain & Co. Ltd of Cardiff is considered the 'National Brewer of Wales', and the company was formed in 1882 by Samuel Arthur Brain and his uncle, Benjamin. The brewery which the Brains acquired was actually established in 1713, but since 2000 brewing has taken place in the former Hancock's brewery, close to Cardiff Central railway station. Brains brews a range of cask, keg and bottled beers, with its popular SA Best Bitter having been introduced during the 1950s. SA is made from a blend of pale and crystal malts, while a balancing dryness is imparted by use of Challenger, Goldings and Fuggles hops.

Budweiser, USA

The word 'Bud' has entered the American language almost as a synonym for beer, such is the ubiquity of the brand across the USA. Today owned by AB InBev, Budweiser was actually introduced in 1876 by the Anheuser-Busch Company, formed by Adolphus Busch, a German immigrant to St Louis, Missouri, and his father-in-law, Eberhard Anheuser. Busch travelled widely in Europe studying advances in brewing techniques, and he took home with him the idea of producing a light-bodied, 'Bohemian-style' lager, at a time when most American drinkers consumed darker ales. Thus was Budweiser created, and today the brand accounts for close to half of all beer consumed in the USA.

Budweiser Budvar, Czech Republic

Despite the dominance of AB InBev's Budweiser, there is *another* Budwesier, much lower in profile, brewed in the Czech Republic city of České Budějovice (Budweis in German) and beloved by beer purists. Beer has been brewed in the town since 1265, and the Budějovický Pivovar company was established in 1895 by local businessmen, who soon began to export their beer to the USA. Not surprisingly, long-running disputes over the use of the name 'Budweiser' ensued, but these were partially resolved when the EEC gave Budweiser Budvar 'Protected Geographical Indication' status, and AB InBev now distributes Budweiser Budvar in the USA and a number of other countries.

Carlsberg, Denmark

Now one of the world's top five brewing companies, the first Carlsberg brewery was established by Jacob Christian Jacobsen just outside the city of Copenhagen in 1847, being named after the founder's son, Carl. From the start, Carlsberg brewed lager, and exports commenced in 1868, with the first shipment destined

Carlsberg poster, 1897.

for Scotland. Seven years later, Carlsberg established the first brewery-owned research facility, named the Carlsberg Laboratory. Most of Denmark's Carlsberg is now brewed in the Frederika Brewery in the west of the country, but brewing also takes place in many other nations, including the UK, where a dedicated lager brewery is located in Northampton.

Chimay, Belgium

Chimay is an authentic Trappist beer, brewed in the Abbaye de Scourmont at Chimay in the Ardennes region of Belgium, where a brewery was first established in 1862. It is the most widely available of the seven officially designated Trappist beers. Rouge,

Blanche and Bleue variants are the principal expressions produced, with the copper-coloured Bleue version of the ale – originally introduced as a Christmas beer in 1948 – generally being considered the classic choice. Since 1876, the Cistercian monks of the Abbaye de Scourmont have also been making their own semi-soft cheese, which is an ideal accompaniment to their beers.

Coors, USA

Along with Budweiser and Miller, Coors is one of the best-known beer brands in the U.S., and since a merger with Canadian brewing giant Molson in 2005 it has been produced by what is known as Molson Coors Brewing Company. Coors was established by German brewer Adolph Kuhrs, later Coors, who migrated to the USA and began brewing in Golden, Colorado, with a partner during 1873. Coors's Golden Brewery is now the largest in the world in terms of output, and Coors Light, introduced in 1978, has grown to become one of the top three beers in the USA.

Corona, Mexico

Corona Extra is a 'tropical pilsner' style of lager, produced by Grupo Modelo at several breweries in Mexico. Corona Extra was first brewed in 1926 to celebrate its owner's tenth anniversary in business. Now available in some 160 countries, with exports to Europe commencing in the early 1990s, Corona is the world's best-selling Mexican beer and the leading import brand in both the USA and Canada. Corona is marketed in a clear glass bottle with a label printed on to it, and the distinctive crown – or *corona* – motif is said to represent the crown on the Cathedral of Our Lady of Guadalupe in Puerto Vallarta.

Duvel, Belgium

Duvel is a strong, golden ale brewed in Belgium by members of the fourth generation of the Moortgat family. The company was founded in 1871 by Jan-Leonard Moortgat and his wife, and the Duvel brand was introduced in 1923, initially under the name Victory Ale, in order to celebrate victory over the Germans during the First World War. Legend has it that during initial samplings of the new beer, a local shoemaker, struck by its potent aroma, declared 'This is a real Devil', or '*duvel*' in Flemish, and the name stuck. Originally formulated as a dark beer, Duvel was transformed into a blonde ale in 1970, and is bottle-conditioned.

Erdinger, Germany

Johann Kienle founded a brewery dedicated to the production of wheat beer in the town of Erding, Bavaria, in 1886. After several changes in ownership, the brewery's general manager, Franz Brombach, bought the plant in 1935, going on to rename it Erdinger Weissbräu in 1949. The brewery remains in the hands of the Brombach family, and is one of the largest private brewing concerns in Germany. It is also the country's most prolific producer of wheat beer. Weissbräu is brewed using fine yeast in accordance with the Bavarian Purity Law, and is still bottle-fermented in the traditional way for three to four weeks.

Foster's, Australia

Although hugely successful on the international stage and available in more than 150 countries, Foster's lager is much less ubiquitous in its native Australia than might be imagined. The brand was launched in 1888, two years after Americans W. M. and R. R. Foster had established a state-of-the-art lager brewery in Melbourne. Much of the brand's success has come in the UK, where Foster's debuted during 1972, becoming an instant hit, and the pale lager is now the second-best-selling beer in Britain. Owned by the Foster's Group, Foster's lager is produced in Europe by Heineken International and in the USA by SABMiller plc.

Grolsch, The Netherlands

Grolsch has been brewed in the Netherlands since 1897, and has its origins in a brewery established in the town of Grol in 1615 by Willem Neerfeldt. The premium pilsner is notable for its distinctive, green, swing-top bottle. Since 2008 the Grolsch brand has been owned by what is now SABMiller, and brewing takes place at Usselo, while Grolsch is also produced under licence in the UK. Unlike some of its rivals, Grolsch undergoes a relatively lengthy ten-week period of lagering. Some 50 per cent of all Grolsch is sold in the Netherlands, but the pilsner is available in more than 70 countries.

Guinness, Ireland

In 1759 Arthur Guinness signed a 9,000-year lease on a disused brewery at St James's Gate in Dublin, paying an annual rent of £45, and a decade later the first export (six and a half barrels!) was made to England. By 1833 St James's Gate was the largest brewery in Ireland, and Guinness developed a worldwide reputation. Now owned by Diageo plc, Guinness is brewed in more than 50 countries around the world and is available in over 150 in total. It is estimated that some 10 million glasses of Guinness are consumed every day.

Heineken, The Netherlands

One of the best-known names in the world of beer, Heineken lager was created by Gerard Adriaan Heineken, who bought the late sixteenth-century Den Hoybergh brewery in Amsterdam during

1864, renaming it the Heineken Brewery in 1873. A year later he opened a second brewery in Rotterdam and built a modern replacement for his original Amsterdam plant in 1886. The following year, production switched from ale to lager. Today much domestic brewing takes place at Zoeterwoude, near Leiden, though Heineken International is now the third-largest brewing company in the world in terms of volume, and its lagers are made in more than 125 breweries across 70 countries.

Hoegaarden, Belgium

Monks in the Belgian town of Hoegaarden reputedly developed a recipe for witbier, or white beer, in 1445, and by the nineteenth century the town boasted thirteen breweries. However, the witbier style went out of fashion over time, and the last Hoegaarden brewery, named Tomsin, closed in 1957. Thanks to the efforts of Pierre Celis, however, the witbier style was revived in the town a decade later in a small farmhouse brewery. The 'new' beer was an immediate success and the operation expanded, with what was then Interbrew, now AB InBev, buying it out in 1987. Today Hoegaarden is marketed as 'the original Belgian white beer'.

Kingfisher, India

Kingfisher is the best-selling beer in India, with a market share of more than 36 per cent. It is owned by the United Breweries Group and varieties include Premium, Strong, Ultra – fuller-bodied and intended to compete with imported brands like Heineken and Carlsberg – and Blue, aimed at young, male drinkers. Kingfisher was first brewed during 1857 in Castle Breweries, Mysore, and in 1915 the brewery joined forces with four others in southern India, creating United Breweries. Today the brand is strongly associated with cricket sponsorships and the Sahara Force India Formula 1 motor racing team.

Kronenbourg, France

The most popular variant of Kronenbourg is the pale lager Kronenbourg 1664, and the date refers to the year in which Geronimus Hatt obtained his Master Brewer's certificate and established his Canon Brewery in the Place du Corbeau, Strasbourg, now part of France. Kronenbourg is owned by the Carlsberg Group and its principal brewery is in Obernai, though '1664' is also brewed under licence in the UK by Heineken International and in Australia by the Foster's Group. Kronenbourg 1664 was first brewed in 1952 and is the best-selling premium lager in France, boasting around one-third of the nation's total beer market.

Innis & Gunn, Scotland

Although only launched in 2003, Innis & Gunn's Original Oak Aged Beer and subsequent range extensions have proved remarkably popular both in the UK and export markets. The creation of the beer was accidental, in that Dougal Sharp of Edinburgh's Caledonian Brewery was asked by William Grant & Sons Ltd to develop a beer that could be used to season whisky barrels for an 'ale-cask finish'. The beer was subsequently poured away, until its unique style was eventually recognized. Innis & Gunn is brewed under contract by Tennent's in Glasgow and matured in ex-bourbon barrels for 30 days and then for a further 47 days in a marrying tun.

Labatt, Canada

Labatt was established in 1847, when an Irish migrant by the name of John Kinder Labatt acquired a modest brewery in London, Ontario, and from those humble origins the Labatt Brewing Company Ltd grew into a business that today controls some 40 per cent of the Canadian beer market. Now part of AB InBev, Labatt operates six breweries and is best known for its Labatt Blue brand, originally introduced in 1951 as Labatt Pilsner and rechristened Blue in 1968, having widely been referred to by that nickname due to its blue label. In addition to its own range of products, Labatt brews Budweiser and Guinness for the Canadian market.

Leffe, Belgium

Leffe is an abbey beer, now in the ownership of AB InBev, but with its origins in the Abbaye Notre-Dame de Leffe in Belgium, where brewing commenced during the thirteenth century. Brewing ceased on the premises in 1809 until 1952, when Father Abbot Nys began brewing Leffe Brune ale once again, with the aid of professional brewer Albert Lootvoet. The most widely available variants of Leffe are Blonde and Brune, and production now takes place in the Stella Artois brewery in Leuven; royalties from the beer's sales – in some 60 countries – are paid to the Leffe abbey.

Marston's Pedigree, England

Marston's was founded in Burton upon Trent in 1834 by John Marston, and the brewery moved to its present site, then known as the Albion Brewery, following a merger with John Thompson & Son Ltd in 1898. The company was bought by Wolverhampton & Dudley Breweries plc in 1999, with the name of the enlarged operation being changed to Marston's plc eight years later. Marston's is renowned for its use of a distinctive brewing regime, known as the Burton Union system, which employs oak casks for fermentation. The Pedigree brand was launched as a pale ale in 1952 and is now one of the best-selling ales in the UK.

Newcastle Brown Ale, England

Newcastle Brown Ale has almost legendary status in the north-east of England, having been introduced in 1927 by Newcastle

Breweries Ltd, who produced it at their Tyne Brewery. In 1960, Newcastle Breweries Ltd became part of Scottish & Newcastle Breweries Ltd, and today is in the ownership of Heineken UK. All links with the city of its birth have been lost, with Newcastle Brown Ale now being brewed in the John Smith's brewery at Tadcaster in Yorkshire. Nonetheless, 'Broon', as it often known in the northeast, is exported to more than 40 countries and is the most popular imported beer in the USA.

Peroni, Italy

Peroni is brewed in Italy and is the country's best-known brand of beer, often being lauded as an example of Italian style. The brand was established by Giovanni Peroni in Vigevano in 1846, with brewing moving to Rome in 1864. From this time onwards, Peroni became progressively better known and more popular, and in 2005 the brand was acquired by SABMiller, which has invested heavily in promoting the Peroni Nastro Azzuro expression in more than 50 countries. The Nastro Azzuro variant was introduced in 1963 and is more full-flavoured than the 'standard' Peroni. The name means 'Blue Ribbon' in Italian.

Pilsner Urquell, Czech Republic

First produced in the city of Pilsen, now part of the Czech Republic, in 1842, Pilsner Urquell was the earliest pale lager ever to be brewed. Urquell means 'original source', and it only came into being because the citizens of Pilsen were unhappy with the quality of beer being made in their town, leading to the creation of a new brewery and the hiring of Bavarian brewer Josef Groll to start afresh. The new style of beer achieved instant success both at home and abroad, being on sale in the USA as early as 1873. The Urquell brand is now owned by the SABMiller Group.

Stella Artois, Belgium

Stella Artois is a pilsner owned by AB InBev, which enjoys international sales and is brewed in a number of countries, such as the UK, Australia and Brazil, in addition to its native Belgium. The beer's home is the town of Leuven, where records for Den Horen Brewery date back to 1366. The Artois name was first associated with the brewery in 1717, courtesy of master brewer Sebastian Artois, and 'Stella' Artois was introduced in 1926, originally as a Christmas beer, with exports commencing during 1930. A new, automated brewery at Leuven opened in 1993, and total annual production is now more than 1 billion litres.

Tennent's, Scotland

Historically one of the trinity of major names in Scottish brewing along with McEwan and Younger, Tennent's is now owned by the Irish C&C Group plc. Brothers Robert and Hugh Tennent established the Drygate Brewery close to Glasgow Cathedral in 1740, though brewing on the site actually dated back to 1556. The brewery was subsequently renamed Wellpark, and lager was first produced there in 1885, with a dedicated lager brewery being constructed between 1889 and 1891. Tennent's lager is the market leader in Scotland and something of a national institution. For many years, cans of Tennent's featured pictures of female models, popularly known as 'lager lovelies'.

Tetley's, England

With great mass-market British beer brands such Bass and Whitbread having withered to a shadow of their former selves, Tetley's remains to wave the flag for English beers, with origins deep in the nineteenth century. Joshua Tetley founded his brewery at Leeds in Yorkshire in 1822, and after numerous amalgamations and takeovers, Tetley's ultimately became part of the Carlsberg

Group in 1998. The historic Tetley's Brewery in Leeds was closed in 2011, with brewing of products such as the original Tetley's Bitter and the popular Smoothflow now being outsourced to other breweries. Over 100 million pints of Tetley's were sold during 2011.

Tiger, Singapore

Tiger beer was launched in 1932 as part of a joint venture between Heineken and Singapore-based Fraser & Neave. Originally known as Malayan Breweries, the business now trades as Asia Pacific Breweries. Its flagship Tiger pale lager is brewed in eleven countries across Asia, with India being the most recent to gain a Tiger brewery. Overall, Tiger is available in more than 60 international markets, and Asia Pacific Breweries actually operates 30 breweries in a dozen nations. Tiger is brewed using yeast cultured in the

Tiger beer van, Bangkok.

Netherlands, while rice is added to the malted barley content to produce a relatively dry finish.

Tsingtao, China

English and German colonists set up the Anglo-German Brewery Co. Ltd and built what is China's oldest brewery, named Tsingtao, in Qingdao (historically Tsingtao) in Shandong province in 1903. German brewing techniques were employed to create a lager that was soon winning awards, and today Tsingtao is available in over 60 countries around the world. Indeed, it accounts for more than 50 per cent of China's total beer exports, and is the leading branded consumer product exported from the country. Tsingtao has been available since 1972 in the USA, where it is the best-selling Chinese beer. While there were just four Tsingtao breweries in 1996, that number has now expanded to a remarkable 48.

Select Bibliography

Barnard, Alfred, *The Noted Breweries of Great Britain and Ireland*
     (London, 1889–91)
Barnett, Paul, *Beer: Facts, Figures and Fun* (London, 2006)
Cole, Melissa, *Let Me Tell You about Beer* (London, 2011)
Eames, Alan D., *The Secret Life of Beer* (North Adams, MA, 2005)
Evans, Jeff, *The Book of Beer Knowledge* (St Albans, 2004)
Glover, Brian, *Beer: An Illustrated History* (London, 1997)
Gourvish, T. R., and R. G. Wilson, *The British Brewing Industry,
     1830–1980* (Cambridge, 1994)
Hackwood, Frederick, *Inns, Ales and Drinking Customs of Old
     England* (London, 1909)
Halley, Ned, *Dictionary of Drink* (Ware, Hertfordshire, 2005)
Jackson, Michael, ed., *Beer* (London, 2007)
—, ed., *The World Guide to Beer* (London, 1977)
Mosher, Randy, *Tasting Beer* (North Adams, MA, 2009)
Nelson, Larry, ed., *The Brewery Manual 2012* (Reigate, Surrey, 2012)
Oliver, Garrett, ed., *The Oxford Companion to Beer* (Oxford, 2012)
Smith, Gavin D., *British Brewing* (Thrupp, Gloucestershire, 2004)
Tierney-Jones, Adrian, ed., *1001 Beers You Must Try Before You
     Die* (London, 2010)
Van Damme, Jaak, and Hilde Deweer, *All Belgian Beers*
     (Oostkamp, 2011)
Webb, Tim, and Joris Pattyn, *100 Belgian Beers to Try Before You
     Die* (St Albans, 2008)
Yenne, Bill, *Beers of the World* (London, 1994)

Websites, Associations, Festivals and Museums

Websites and Publications

Beer Advocate (USA)
beeradvocate.com

Beer and Brewer (Australia)
beerandbrewer.com

Beer Connoisseur (USA)
beerconnoisseur.com

Beer Magazine (USA)
thebeermag.com

Beer Pages
beer-pages.com

Brauwelt (Germany)
brauwelt.de

Brewer's Guardian (UK)
brewersguardian.com

Craft Beer (USA)
craftbeer.com

Modern Brewery Age (USA)
breweryage.com

Real Beer
realbeer.com

What's Brewing (UK)
camra.org.uk

World Beer Awards
worldbeerawards.com

Associations

Beer Institute (USA)
beerinstitute.org

Belgian Brewers Association
beerparadise.be

Campaign for Real Ale (CAMRA)
camra.org.uk

European Beer Consumers Union
ebcu.org

North American Brewers Association
northamericanbrewers.org

Society of Independent Brewers
siba.co.uk

Festivals

American Craft Beer Week
craftbeer.com

Beerfest Asia (Singapore)
beerfestasia.com

Bruges Beer Festival (Bruges, Belgium)
brugesbierfestival.be

Great American Beer Festival (Denver, CO)
greatamericanbeerfestival.com

Great British Beer Festival (London)
gbbf.camra.org.uk

Great Canadian Beer Festival (Victoria, BC)
gcbf.com

Great Japan Beer Festival (Tokyo, Japan)
beertaster.org

New York Craft Beer Week
nycbeerweek.com

Oktoberfest (Munich, Germany)
oktoberfest.de

San Francisco Beer Week
sfbeerfest.com

Museums

Bavarian Brewery Museum (Kulmback, Germany)
bayerisches-brauerimuseum.de

Beer and Oktoberfest Museum (Munich, Germany)
bier-und-oktoberfestmuseum.de

Belgian Brewers Museum (Brussels, Belgium)
beerparadise.be

Brussels Museum of Gueuze (Brussels, Belgium)
cantillon.be

Carlsberg Visitors Centre (Copenhagen, Denmark)
visitcarlsberg.dk

European Beer Museum (Stenay, France)
musee-de-la-bière.com

Guinness Storehouse (Dublin, Ireland)
guinness-storehouse.com

Heineken Experience (Amsterdam, Netherlands)
heinekenexperience.com

National Beer Museum (Alkmaar, Netherlands)
biermuseum.nl

National Brewery Centre (Burton upon Trent, UK)
nationalbrewerycentre.co.uk

Sapporo Beer Museum (Sapporo, Japan)
sapporobeer.jp

The Brewery Museum (Pilsen, Czech Republic)
prazdrojvisit.cz/en

Acknowledgements

Thanks to Amy Brice, British Pub & Beer Association, David Burkhart, Tom Cannavan, David Cross, Neal Gruer of AB InBev, John Humphreys of Shepherd-Neame, Tony Johnson of Fullers, Laura Overton of Brains, Roger Protz, Rupert Ponsonby, Eibhlin Roche of Diageo, Rory Steel.

Photo Acknowledgements

The author and the publishers wish to express their thanks to the below sources of illustrative material and/or permission to reproduce it.

Author's collection: pp. 28, 40, 41, 59, 71, 73, 79, 82, 85; © The Trustees of the British Museum: pp. 23, 58, 62, 109; Carlsberg Group: p. 137; Thongpool Chantarak 'Da': p. 146; Photo by Luca Galuzzi – www.galuzzi.it: p. 45; Hofbräuhaus, Munich: pp. 53 (BBMC Tobias Razinger), 86; iStockphoto: pp. 37 (helovi), 70 (pjohnson1), 75 (ShutterWorx), 76 (chang); Library of Congress, Washington, DC: pp. 30, 56, 67, 68, 69, 72; Shutterstock: pp. 6 (Sergey Peterman), 10 (Antonio Abrignani), 16 (Neftali), 21 (Oleg Golovnev), 22 (Morphart Creation), 29 (chippix), 36 (sgm), 38 (Claudine Van Massenhove), 39 (Daniel Rajszczak), 52 (filmfoto), 77 (Andreas Juergensemeier), 78 (Martin D. Vonka), 87 (chippix), 92 (Claudio Divizia), 93 (Tyler Panian), 95 (Thierry Dagnelie), 98 (Alexey U), 112 (Chris Green), 116 (Tupungato), 117 (Action Sports Photography), 147 (TonyV3112); E. Michael Smith (Chiefio): p. 12; Victoria & Albert Museum, London: p. 94; Vistor7: p. 31.

Index

italic numbers refer to illustrations; **bold** to recipes